The *Other Game* of Golf

The *Other Game* of Golf

Practical Principles & Strategies for Business on the Course.

by

J. Brian Amster, Larry Salk,
and
Craig Lockwood

toExcel
San Jose   New York   Lincoln   Shanghai

The Other Game of Golf
Practical Principles & Strategies for Business on the Course.

All Rights Reserved. Copyright © 1999 by *Golf Resource Group*

Illustrations by Michael Jacques

No part of this book may be reproduced or transmitted in any form or by any means, graphic, electronic, or mechanical, including photocopying, recording, taping, or by any information storage or retrieval system, without the permission in writing from the publisher.

This edition published by toExcel Press, an imprint of iUniverse.com, Inc.

For information address:
iUniverse.com, Inc.
620 North 48th Street
Suite 201
Lincoln, NE 68504-3467
www.iuniverse.com

ISBN: 1-58348-350-0

LCCN: 99-66327

Contents

Foreword vi

Introduction viii

Part I   The Elements of Form 1

Chapter 1
Seven basic principles of playing golf's "other game" 3

1. "Other game" players play the business game. 5
2. "Other game" golf doesn't demand great skill. 6
3. "Other game" players behave the way they play. 7
4. "Other game" golf's not about competition. 8
5. "Other game" players return to play again. 9
6. "Other game" players heed wise words. 10
7. "Other game" players learn to listen carefully. 11

Chapter 2
Ten principles for beginning "other game" players 13

8. "Other game" players start at the beginning. 15
9. "Other game" players aren't handicapped by handicaps. 16
10. "Other game" players play by the rules. 17
11. "Other game" players don't show off. 18
12. "Other game" players present a clean image. 19
13. "Other game" players keep their gear simple. 20

14. "Other game" players learn from better players. 21
15. "Other game" players refine their techniques. 22
16. "Other game" players understand fashion isn't style. 23
17. "Other game" players avoid the influence. 24

Chapter 3
Seven principles of business golf etiquette and protocol 25

18. "Other game" players observe course etiquette. 27
19. "Other game" players initiate conversation. 28
20. "Other game" players mind their manners. 29
21. "Other game" players strive for harmony. 30
22. "Other game" players are gracious—and tip well. 31
23. "Other game" players avoid giving golf lessons. 32
24. "Other game" players maintain 19th hole decorum. 33

Chapter 4
Nine principles of playing the "other game" 35

25. "Other game" players enjoy walking the course. 37
26. "Other game" players take advantage of cart time. 38
27. "Other game" players regulate pace-of-play. 39
28. "Other game" players play promptly. 40
29. "Other game" players avoid making others wait. 41
30. "Other game" players avoid holdups. 42
31. "Other game" players avoid playing therapist. 43
32. "Other game" players know bad games may have good results. 44
33. "Other game" players avoid initiating business discussions. 45

Chapter 5
Seven principles of social strategy 47

34. "Other game" players are social initiators. 48
35. "Other game" players are don't wanters. 49

36. "Other game" players love an enthusiastic player. 50
37. "Other game" players avoid becoming golf introverts. 51
38. "Other game" players are alert for opportunity. 52
39. "Other game" players avoid defining wants as needs. 53
40. "Other game" players observe their partners' playing levels. 54

Chapter 6
Five principles of the "other game's" inner game 55

41. "Other game" players define themselves as magicians. 57
42. "Other game" players make arrangements in advance. 58
43. "Other game" players call the pro beforehand. 59
44. "Other game" players befriend starters and caddiemasters. 60
45. "Other game" players avoid economic surprises. 61

Part II   Putting Golf's "Other Game" Into Play 63

Chapter 7
"When the student is ready the teacher appears." 65

Chapter 8
Practice, practice, practice 67

Chapter 9
Into the game—feet first 69

Chapter 10
Provisions for the journey 71

Chapter 11
Correct attire for the "other game" 75

Chapter 12
Correct women's attire for the "other game" 79

Chapter 13
Words of wardrobe wisdom 81

Chapter 14
Zen and the art of "other game" maintenance 85

Chapter 15
Keeping "other game" behavior on course 87

Chapter 16
Game combinations, clubs and courses 89

Chapter 17
Join a club 91

Chapter 18
Prestigious Golf Clubs Observe Formal Rules 95

Chapter 19
Prestigious Golf and Country Clubs' 19th Holes 97

Chapter 20
Wagering 99

Chapter 21
Tournaments—How and Why They Work For "Other Game" Players 103

Chapter 22
Tipping Caddies 107

Chapter 23
Pace-of-play and Other Important Factors 109

Chapter 24
Establishing Your Handicap 111

Chapter 25
Putting Promotes Points 113

Chapter 26
Why Golf Was Made For Walking 115

Chapter 27
Ensuring Prompt Play.. 117

Chapter 28
Drinking, Smoking, and Eating on the Course 119

Chapter 29
What To Do When Your Playing Partner Needs a
Psychotherapist 121

Chapter 30
Invitation and Reciprocation 123

Epilogue... 127

About the Authors.. 129

Foreword

The **Other Game** *of Golf* is an amusing and helpful book for anyone interested in the social and business aspects of a golf outing. Personally, I started playing golf relatively late in life, purely as a recreational activity that I could share with my Dad who—having been a Depression-era kid from New York City—discovered the game quite late in his life as well.

We both found the game to be one of the best escapes imaginable from the hustle and bustle of busy business schedules and city life. At the same time, neither one of us had grown up being members of country clubs and knowing the niceties of what the authors refer to as the "other game" of golf.

The **Other Game** *of Golf* focuses on how personal relationships can be strengthened from a round or two of golf. This bonding process has implications for business relationships on many levels. You actually get to see how someone reacts to both good fortune and adversity, and since so often minor bets or pride bets are part of the golf ritual, you also get to see how someone reacts under pressure, or handles letting down the team in tournament play.

This "other game" of golf has nothing to with your handicap or how well you score. It does have to do with how you play the game. Do you lose your temper and get irritable? Do you applaud or ignore the good play of your partners and competitors? Do you focus on the game at hand, or try to do a deal? Do you respect the etiquette of the game?

These are not minor considerations, and can greatly impact the experience of golf for you and your playing partners. I often play golf alone, just for the pleasure of the game and being outdoors, but when playing with others I am likely to also have business or potential business relationship with my playing partners or opponents. Had a copy of *The* **Other Game** *of Golf* been available sooner for such occasions, I would have benefited enormously. Although I eventually learned through trial-and-error most of what *The* **Other Game** *of*

Golf explains, it took over ten years of business golf outings and occasional stress over not knowing exactly what to do, and when.

If *The **Other Game** of Golf* can eliminate even one of these trial-and-error moments for you, it is well worth the quick and enjoyable hour read. It will also serve as a reference to which you may return again, and again.

Enjoy this book, enjoy your golf, and may your business and professional life flourish.

William Gladstone,
Cardiff-by-the-Sea, California
January, 1999

William Gladstone is a passionate mid-handicap player and successful literary agent and publishing/information/training broker.

Introduction

The **Other Game** *of Golf: Practical Principles & Strategies For Business On the Course*, is not a book of "tips" or "how to's," but a "when you" book, a trustworthy companion, written as a reference for both novice and experienced players.

This little book is designed to help you understand the subtle elements that characterize the complex game of business golf—the game we euphemistically call the "other game"—and what to do *when* you decide to practice and play golf's "other game."

While golf tip and teaching texts abound, *The* **Other Game** *of Golf* isn't focused on how to hit a ball, select equipment, or get around a golf course. We offer only a very few, and very limited recommendations.

Instead, we've defined and organized a series of 45 easily recalled one-sentence principles that will enable you to create and function within a sophisticated business-golf environment—projecting a high level of perceived performance—regardless of your personal level of playing-skill.

The **Other Game** *of Golf* provides you with the previously uncollected rules of the business game—an adroit synthesis of strategic social, and tactical psychological skills that you can refer to, and use.

This little book underscores the importance of understanding the unwritten protocols developed, refined, and practiced by generations of business players.

Well before the American Revolution, the British aristocracy—rich and powerful men—found the "links" as they were referred to then, a perfect venue upon which to discuss their fortunes, kingdoms, empires, and loves, without distractions, and well away from prying eyes and eavesdropping ears. Gentlemen still do.

Over the last 25 years, however, and especially today, businesswomen have also discovered the benefits of playing business golf as a valuable adjunct to their careers.

Women executives are finding that a strategically wielded golf club is the perfect tool with which to chip away and drive through the so-called "glass ceiling." Playing this "other game" of golf, which demands a keen eye for when, where, and with whom to play, puts them on an equal footing with their male colleagues in terms of time spent with corporate and business decision-makers.

*The **Other Game** of Golf* identifies certain unwritten components which are compatible with enhancing business relationships, and organizes these observations into a set of easily recalled one-sentence principles dealing with the psychological and social aspects of the "other game."

Consider golf, for instance, in terms of time alone. Where else would you have time to be with an important decision-maker or client, away from distractions, for more than four hours?

For this reason savvy business people and statesmen have used golf as a valuable mechanism for expanding relationships with other important and influential people.

Golf has become a dominant part of the executive's panoply because it provides astute players insights in a few hours which might never arise during the normal course of business.

Unfortunately, there's a catch; getting a proper education about the "other game's" unwritten principles is not easy. Some of the information is arcane, esoteric—passed down, father-or-mother-to-son or daughter, by example at exclusive country clubs and elite prep-school and university golf teams—and never, never written down.

These "elements of form"—which have nothing to do with your score—enhance rapid career advancement by allowing "other game" players to negate restrictive formal corporate and political hierarchies, while mastering their discriminating social behaviors.

This is where *The **Other Game** of Golf* comes in—organizing those unwritten dicta of business-golf, including subtle aspects of etiquette, wagering, and the judicious use of the cart or caddie to advantage—into a set of classic, practical principles.

The **Other Game** *of Golf* invites you to put down your misconceptions and pick up your clubs—teeing off to improve your bottom-line—in social skills, status and income.

J. Brian Amster
Larry Salk
Craig Lockwood

PART I

The Elements of Form

Forty-five practical principles
for playing the "other game" of golf.

Chapter 1

Seven basic principles of playing golf's "other game."

Have you ever considered what makes golf, played for business purposes, superior to power breakfasts or lunches, or even face-to-face meetings?

Golf is the only major land game or sport, with the possible exception of certain kinds of hunting, in which players embark on a safe, formalized journey and interact in a relaxed setting for long periods of time.

But golf's journey differs greatly from the way playing partners, especially women and men, interact in any other active sport such as tennis, bowling, running or other court sports.

And what a journey it is. Tiger Woods, a young man few had heard of before he won the Masters, was invited shortly after his victory to play with President William Jefferson Clinton. While he declined the invitation, perhaps fearing that he might be used for political purposes, he may not have realized that golfing with the President of the United States—and *being* used for political purposes—is an important American tradition.

Starting with President Dwight D. Eisenhower, golf on a Presidential level has always been considered the most prestigious of invitations. During the following presidential administrations, the ultimate golf invitation was playing with the President at Camp David in Virginia.

Presidents from Ike to Bill have extolled golf's ability to help them relax. Indeed, golf may allow presidents to relax, but it also affords them an opportunity to get closer to key political, financial, and business figures.

Receiving a formal invitation bearing the Great Seal of the President of United States of America, post-marked from the White House, regardless of your particular party affiliation, means much more than playing a game of golf for relaxation.

This is the apex of the "other game" of golf. Put simply, it means access to the world's most important figures—in a relaxing environment.

Republican, Democrat, Libertarian, Independent—whatever your political stripe, playing with Ike, Jack, Gerry, Ronnie or Bill was and will continue to be unquestionably the most prestigious invitation any golfer can receive.

That's why historically so many important business, economic and academic people play golf. They cherish the idea of uninterrupted recreation in beautiful outdoor settings, in the company of peers.

On the course, any conversation you may have with an old or potential client is subtly altered by the fact that your respective handicaps have leveled the playing field

Along with this is the enhanced quality of intimacy—without the formality of an office, board or conference room or even a restaurant. On a golf course, you have four hours to discuss a proposal, not 15 minutes.

Even when a deal-obstructing impasse is reached, opportunities for conversation are still limitless—you can always switch to discussing the merits of courses, clubs, balls, and the latest personalities and their innovations in technique. In an office setting you'd have to close your briefcase, shake hands and leave the room. Here you can continue the conversation, and by so doing, increase the potential to continue your relationship—without closing any doors behind you, and in fact opening many more you had never anticipated opening.

Principle #1
"Other game" players play the business game.

Experienced business players will tell you golf is the single-most significant game business people play.

Where else can one spend hours uninterrupted, establish and fortify strong business relationships, develop more intimate and lasting social ties, and learn more about your playing partner?

Court games like tennis separate players with a net. Squash or racquetball are paced too quickly for conversation. Players may be separated because of greatly differing levels of skill and age.

Golf, however, provides an opportunity for business people of all ages, genders and levels of skill to play, compete, bond, relate and exercise—in a collegial, informal manner.

A round of golf allows you to get closer to fellow players than anywhere else. You and your partners soon learn—without a word being spoken—that what you're seeing is probably what you'll be getting.

Played out-of-doors, in constantly changing climatic conditions, golf tends to pit player vs. him-or-herself, vs. the elements, vs. other players. While the potential for ego-conflict is reduced, there is no hiding out. Because of these factors, golf is a wonderful way to observe how the people with whom you are considering doing business operate.

Principle #2
"Other game" golf doesn't demand great skill.

Impressive golf-playing skill is not a prerequisite for playing golf's "other game."

What is appreciated and judged, far beyond physical skill, is your presentation of yourself as an acomplished and secure individual. This means having a good knowledge of course rules, proper course-etiquette, when and where to engage other players in conversation, humor, patience, and playing a prompt, well-paced, acceptable game.

Principle #3
"Other game" players behave the way they play.

It's axiomatic in business circles that people play golf the way they tend to conduct business.

Business people perceive a golfer's playing style to be a probable reflection of their business practices and ethics.

One of the reasons that business people have expanded the use of golf is that it provides unparalleled opportunities for character observation under unique pressure situations.

Driving requires performance in front of a group; shooting from the fairway or the rough allows the business golfer to observe if the other player's game is as good as he claimed; making or missing money putts, taking gimmies, time in the cart—each allows the canny business golfer to observe a potential client or associate's character.

Playing good golf is a strong measure of a person's perceived business capacity. The business golfer who exhibits patience, the ability to clear away extraneous thoughts, to focus on hitting the ball, has acquired skills appreciated by golfing colleagues. Those who always demand gimmies may expect and want favors. Those who exaggerate handicaps, or are unable to accurately count strokes may cheat, con or scam.

Whoever they are, and whatever their personality type, it will manifest in a round of golf.

Principle #4

"Other game" golf's not about competition.

While there is a strong competitive spirit to golf, business golf more properly embraces the collegial aspects of social interaction.

In golf's "other game," it's important to remember that your partners will remember their experience with you on the course—good or bad.

This brings into play the what, when, where, and why of golf's "other game."

Golf, as in business, may be measured and followed statistically, but beyond numbers on a scorecard it is a game of nerves and vision, a game where players can bluff their way into your head, and of course, there is always a winner and a loser.

The game is rarely mastered, but more importantly, it can be enjoyed for the day and the moment, knowing it will be equally challenging the next time. Fortunately, a golfer's last game has no bearing on the next game.

Golf's "other game" is a game of and for life. What other sport could we enjoy competitively with someone many years, or even generations, younger or older? And what other sport can be played equally by both sexes for as long as health and interest hold?

Principle #5

"Other game" players return to play again.

Fundamental to golf's "Other game" is the principle that spending a day on the course with interesting playing partners is the best way to establish and fortify strong business relationships.

Business people tend to be a varied lot, the best of whom didn't develop materially without significant effort at developing interests on a corresponding social, cultural, and intellectual level. They like and seek relationships with interesting people from whom they can learn, and broaden their own networks.

Discussion during a round may center on subjects tangent to business, or veer away from business—only to come back.

This doesn't mean you must to be able to discuss de Kooning's contributions to Abstract Expressionism, or expound on e.e. cummings's typographical symbolism in American poetry the first time out.

On a practical level, however, your "other game" will always benefit by an intellectual curiosity about—if not a command of—a broad range of areas beyond your given profession or business, including art, music, and literature. Intelligent curiosity is, after all, a characteristic of cultured people.

And even if the business you had hoped to conduct doesn't occur as a result of this round, if you are interested and interesting, you will be sought after in the future.

Principle #6

"Other game" players heed wise words.

"I believe that if someone really wants a happy life, then it is very important to pursue both internal and external means; in other words, material development and mental development."

His Holiness, the XIV Dalai Lama.

We don't know if the Dalai Lama plays golf. He is an affable, intelligent, charming and very dedicated man with a good sense of humor, and we have no doubts that he would make a wonderful playing partner. He wears a sleeveless maroon robe which would give him plenty of swing room.

The point we're making here is that any material development you're striving to achieve through your business is best achieved by developing your social, emotional, intellectual and even spiritual skills. These will become an intrinsic part of your "other game," as they become part of your life.

Principle #7
"Other game" players learn to listen carefully.

When you use golf as a tool to enhance *business* relationships, treat the round as a means of creating stronger *personal* relationships with your playing partners.

This is the essence of the "other game."

As your previous business experience—on or off the course—may have already shown you, there are no right words, or formulas for creating the opening for a business discussion to begin. If there were, they would be known and this book would be unnecessary. This, however, is where intuition, "feel," and your personal interest in your playing partner comes in.

Finding commonality between players requires two basic communication skills—*speaking* and *listening*.

Your playing partner or partners may be very open to discussing business, or they may not. You'll need to discover their preferences and then proceed accordingly.

Finishing a round, changing focus from on-course discussions of pin placement to private placement will seem much easier, because you and your playing partner have just conquered, or been conquered by the course.

Over a cool drink or warm meal you can sense how your relationship has progressed. It's a simple matter to change focus from the game to the relationship.

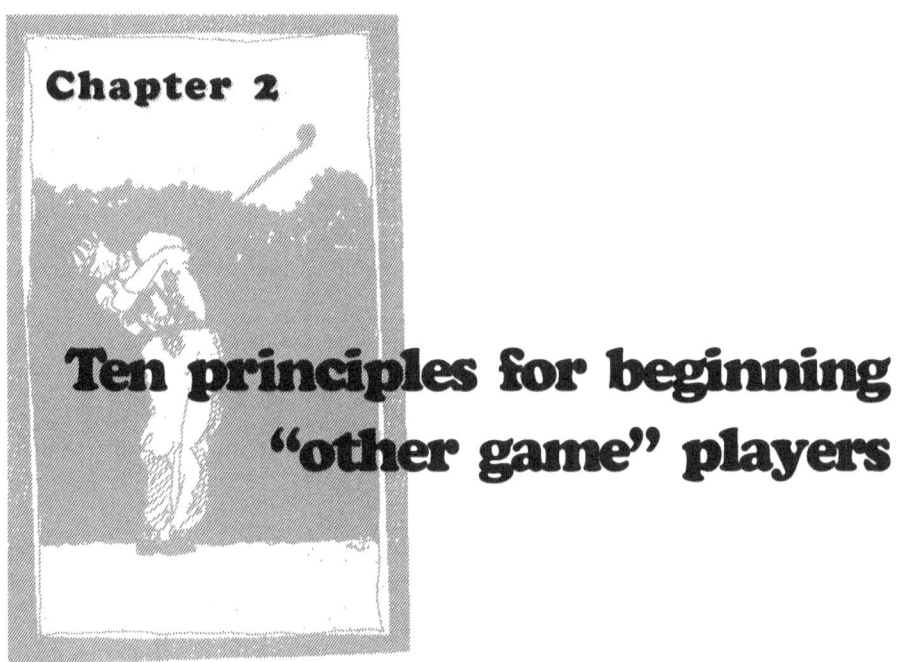

Chapter 2

Ten principles for beginning "other game" players

Learn and practice flexibility; golf, as does business, demands adapting to changing conditions.

Good golfers understand that no two rounds of golf are ever the same—chance is your unseen partner in every round.

Each situation, each shot, requires a new approach and strategy. You may land in the same trap, but pin placement can increase or decrease the degree of playing difficulty. Wind and humidity, things you can't see, affect each shot. Greens can be fast or slow, hard or soft. Morning dew, or a light drizzle will demand great player adaptability.

Obstructive tree branches may interfere one day, but be gone the next. Balls may land—anywhere.

Nor are any two business games ever the same. You'll change roles—from sponsor of the day, to guest—necessitating a quick assessment of the conventions governing each situation. But you can have an edge by understanding how to see the elements, turning an ordinary business game into an "other game."

Golf is a sport of character—far more mental than physical. In his book *Golf in the Kingdom*, Michael Murphy's character Shivas Irons mentions *"...that all one has to do is concentrate on the little white ball for two- and one-half seconds."*

True—but easier said than done.

And here is where the elements of chance intervene.

First tee jitters? Shank one in the fairway? Dump one in the bunker? Knock one into the water? Jack a four-footer?

Play by the "American rules"—one mulligan off the tee and two in the fairway per nine? How about "winter rules"—improving the ball's lie in the fairway? What about the 4-foot gimmie putt? Or how about the gimmie putt half-heartedly attempted by one-arming it, only to lip out—not counted?

All the golfer's reactions when chance interdicts to change the way a game's going can be translated into how one reacts in business.

Are you a gracious and thoughtful host? Do you generate positive conversation in the cart when your playing partner's having a tough day, or game? Do you improve your lies with a little bump in the rough? Do you count all your strokes?

Your "other game" partners will observe your actions under chance conditions and judge you.

Business golfers who have learned to play the "other game" listen, observe, and respond to everything chance drops into their surroundings. Their partners, the course, themselves. They listen as they would like to be heard.

And they always understand that all chance reactions produce equal—and often fortuitous—reactions.

Principle #8

"Other game" players start at the beginning.

Once you've decided to play golf's "other game" you'll need provisions for the journey.

Don't start buying equipment.

Buy a golf rule-book.

Familiarize yourself with the rules and terminology, and learn how golf is played.

Golf, just as business, has complex rules. Experienced players, especially corporate business players, exist in a sometimes-rigid corporate culture of policies and protocols. This consciousness of rule, structure and decorum accompanies them to their golf games.

Avoid attempting to be seen as an expert. Expect to be playing with more experienced players from whom you can learn.

Your first objective—and the key to immediate acceptance—is simply being seen as a person who is relaxed on a golf course and is familiar with the rules.

Principle # 9

"Other game" players aren't handicapped by handicaps.

Golf has always been recognized as a universal sport due in part to the "handicap"—a device allowing the equalization of the game between players of differing levels of strength and skill.

This concept is critical since there is an immediate understanding when one player states her handicap as "ten" and the other reports his is "twenty-two."

Because of this singular factor, golf has emerged as *the* game of business players. With the handicap in place, business professionals can center their efforts on becoming comfortable with each other while playing from their own levels of skill.

For the "other game" player, a handicap's never a handicap.

Principle #10
"Other game" players play by the rules.

Golf is a rule-bound game, and playing means playing by the rules.

There are many rules to suit the many kinds of situations and conditions a player encounters. The solution, as we suggested earlier, are rule books. They are small, inexpensive, and easy to read.

A quick glance will help clarify or solve a dilemma. When you are stymied and your fellow players are unable to offer solutions, rules function to clarify the game. Understand and play according to them.

Golfers encounter a wide spectrum of elements as well as the infinite number of varying circumstances. The only way to determine if you are getting better—as opposed to just hitting a ball—is to play inside the game's rules.

Remember, people will notice how you *play* the game, not necessarily what you shoot, or score.

Principle #11

"Other game" players don't show off.

An inept boor can buy the best of clubs and bags. And many do. All it takes is enough money.

Clubs are one obvious, but not necessarily accurate, key to assessing the "other game" golfer. Be very careful about stereotyping and rendering final judgments.

Arriving to tee off with a dirty, jumbled set of mismatched clubs, certainly at some level creates a strong personal impression.

Old, grubby, shabby clubs are indicative of someone who takes the game less than seriously—as compared to a complete set of nicely matched woods and irons.

There is always the chance, however, that the player with the terrible set of clubs is a great golfer. Perhaps his clubs were misplaced in transit and he's cobbled together an emergency set. Suddenly those old clubs indicate a resourceful individual, unfazed by the exigencies of contemporary travel, and so confident of his or her skill that they'll play with whatever they can find for the sheer joy and love of the game.

If this is the case, they'll probably relate a humorous anecdote. If not, the player's handicap will be the next signpost you'll encounter.

Should you find yourself facing a scratch player with a bag of "auld spoons" and a 1-iron, or some discount-store specials, be reticent, and consult our section on wagering.

Principle #12

"Other game" players present a clean image.

Always strive to create a clean, simple image: avoid gaudy clothing and equipment.

Savvy business golfers soon develop an awareness of appropriate gear. They examine their peers, and assess their images—and how that image works, either for or against them within their business circles. They quickly learn to avoid a patched-together look.

Creating a professional "business" appearance isn't about spending money. It is more properly a matter of careful shopping and selection.

Golf equipment includes the following: clubs, club covers, bag, balls, shoes, gloves. There are also the miscellaneous items you'll appreciate having or—more importantly—being able to lend to your companions should they need them throughout the course of a round.

Your personal presentation, however, is limited to shoes, slacks, cap and shirt, bag and clubs. Here, as we've noted before—keep it simple. Solid colors, well-matched, will never fail you. Avoid overly fashionable, trendy attire in favor of good-quality comfortable garments.

Principle #13

"Other game" players keep their gear simple.

Without an adequate set of clubs, your potential to play reasonable "other game" golf is limited, but the key adjective in this sentence is *adequate*.

Purchase only what you need to start.

Avoid going overboard.

Improve your clubs as you improve your skills.

You will have ample opportunity, once you start taking lessons, playing regularly, and spending time speaking with more experienced players.

If you're a beginning player, select clubs at a reasonable cost, making sure they are designed for durability, and consistency.

As your level of skill improves, reevaluate your equipment, discuss your needs with your pro, and adjust according to your new skills.

Remember: the best is bad enough.

For this reason, choose name brands.

Principle #14

"Other game" players learn from better players.

For beginners, taking lessons is a key to accelerating the learning curve, developing good form, and acceptable competency.

Choose a local golf course, or one recommended by a friend whom you consider a good player, and get to know the teaching professional. Once you have found the pro you feel comfortable with, sign-up for beginning group classes or a multi-lesson plan.

Initially, you'll need to develop the rudimentary skills of correct body position and foot-placement, how to grip your club and the elements of the swing. These components constitute *form*, and in the beginning you'll be better-served by developing good fundamental form than any other aspect of the game.

Yes, it's true that some athletically gifted people play acceptable golf with poor form. But the key to this kind of player is the athletic gift. A beginner of average athletic skill who establishes a strong foundation of correct form will eventually improve—and will find that whatever native athletic skills s/he has will be assisted by good form.

We stress that it's imperative not to develop bad and potentially difficult-to-correct habits—so we strongly recommend you opt for lessons first.

Principle #15

"Other game" players refine their techniques.

Studying any discipline requires discipline.

Golf's "other game" is a subtle discipline, and each level at which you play can be refined. This means everything—from the way you walk on the course, to handling your clubs, setting your tees—every possible aspect of your game.

If you want to develop competency and skill at the game simply acknowledge that this requires constant attention and a good teacher.

Be realistic. Avoid looking for quick fixes or cures for your game.

Principle #16
"Other game" players understand fashion isn't style.

Golf fashions are temporary, while *style* is enduring.

Fashion is what the general public accepts and wears during a certain time-period. Fashion is what clothing merchandisers push as "new" each season.

"Style," noted the Earl of Chesterfield, "is the dress of thoughts."

Style is a combination of subtle characteristics that almost defy description. Style reflects a certain distinctive mode of personal taste, a combination, or *manner* in which articles of clothing are worn. Style is truly an aspect of individual expression, *without* regard to fashion. Indeed, fashion can often be antithetical to a well-developed sense of style

Remember, you are playing for *business*. Be appropriate to the dress standards of your industry, or profession. When in doubt adjust toward the conservative. Understatement can't be overemphasized.

Principle #17

"Other game" players avoid the influence.

For initial business golf meetings, avoid over-indulging in alcoholic beverages. If you are seeking to make an impression, you'll gain more with dry wit than three dry Martinis.

Enjoying an adult beverage on the course is acceptable as long as it doesn't violate course rules, and your partners are not put off by it. But be aware of who your playing partners are, and their personal attitudes toward alcohol.

Religious individuals who hold strongly orthodox views may be made uncomfortable by as much as a bottle of beer. Those recovering from substance abuse could become uncomfortable as well. In the event a partner has brought a minor along, your ability to set a good example by abstaining—at least until the 19th hole—will be an accommodation most parents will appreciate.

Golf's "other game" requires keeping your wits about you. You're not here to unwind, but to have fun while establishing and fostering stronger personal relationships.

Chapter 3

Seven principles of business golf etiquette and protocol

Golf's "other game" is a construct of manners.

Students and players of the "other game," are aware of, and careful to observe, certain basic commonsense elements of golf etiquette.

Etiquette, whether at the dinner-table or on the putting green, is simply a series of ritualized, consensual patterns of behavior. We all tacitly agree that by observing these rituals we can interact socially with a minimum of friction and dispute.

Golf has developed a courtly demeanor over many centuries and many, many millions of hours of play. Business golf observes all of the standard rules of golf etiquette, and has added a few of its own.

Important to understanding golf's "other game" is that what you lack in golf-playing skill will pass unnoticed if you have mastered golf's complex behavioral skills.

For the business golfer, gracefully observed etiquette announces to your golfing companions that you not only know the rules, and play by them, but that you can probably be trusted to comport yourself in a like manner off the course as well.

There are numerous ways to score on the course, and lots of ways to hit a golf ball well. But your mission in playing the "other game" is taking the emphasis off yourself and putting it on how the other players can enjoy the game and get to know you as a kindred soul and spirit.

Again, the "other game" isn't about winning or losing. Successful business people win everyday, and they love it. But they lose as well—and they learn from their mistakes and losses—and thus in losing gain understanding. And they also love this.

So, if the winds are right and the gods of the greens are smiling and you happen to win, they can probably handle losing a match. And if they can't, a disgruntled loser always wants a rematch, so chances are you're assured another golf game and perhaps their business as well.

Principle #18

"Other game" players observe course etiquette.

Golf traditionally requires behaving with dignity, courtesy, respect, and observing strict golf course etiquette.

Course etiquette doesn't include acting with an effete, snotty display of prissy mannerisms. It isn't about correcting other's mistakes.

Course etiquette means behaving with skillful, good-humored consideration for the wants, needs, and comfort of others, in a variety of situations, and changing conditions.

Etiquette, on and off the golf course, is a means of *making others feel at ease*, paying attention, and avoiding social discomfort.

Principle #19

"Other game" players initiate conversation.

Developing interesting conversations, is the "other game's" primary tactic.

Conversation, when shared, establishes levels of familiarity and comfort, which in turn help create relationships.

But this doesn't mean becoming a Master of Ceremonies, dominating the conversational flow, or spewing out arcane factoids—it means encouraging *mutual* responses.

Practicing the "other" game requires honoring the unspoken wishes of the other players by not forcing conversation, and thereby the game itself, off the conversational fairway.

Developing a relationship with other golfers during the course of a round is a key principle to profitable business golf, and the foundation that allows eventual success. This means keeping up lively, but *appropriate* and *stimulating* conversation.

On a personal level, it means that you make a practice of keeping informed about a variety of contemporary subjects that may, at some point, lead you into the *business subject* you most wish to discuss.

Avoid any inclination to discuss business until someone else brings it up. Be mindful that your business here is to establish a relationship—first and foremost.

Principle #20

"Other game" players mind their manners.

Good "other game" golfers are respectful, focused, and observant.

Skillful "other game" golfers are always considerate. They remain still when someone is hitting; replace divots; rake bunkers; hit promptly when it's their turn. And they play prompt golf.

Considerate golfers never patronize another player, nor would they "lay down"—lose on purpose—during a golf round.

"Other game" golfers know that bringing up business on the first tee is in poor taste and something they'll always attempt to avoid.

In the event a less-skillful player broaches the subject, however, "other game" players never make an issue of this rudeness. They simply smile and quietly redirect the errant player's attention.

These are all basic elements of golf etiquette. There are many more. Remember, the objective of the "other game" is not necessarily to score, but to create better relationships.

Principle #21

"Other game" players strive for harmony.

Conducted in the correct spirit and with the right attitude, business golf is a harmonious social art, a way of "being," as opposed to "acting," much in the way a Zen tea ceremony is conducted, as a graceful expression of sincere interest and consummate skill.

Perceiving golf's "other game" as an activity based on opportunism would be a socially fatal mistake.

It's anything but.

Understanding this principle is key to making ordinary business golf into the "other game." Unless it is practiced in this manner it will be quickly recognized as inauthentic, and believe us, intelligent business people learn early on to spot a con, or see through an act. So behavior must harmonize, must come from sincere interest and motive. When it comes from any other place it is patently transparent.

As Mrs. Lockwood once cautioned: *"Dear, I'm too busy seeing how they play to listen to what they say."*

Rush harmony, compound it with disconsonant motives or ambivalent, discordant attitudes and you turn a potentially gracious and enjoyable game into a low-level scam.

Principle #22

"Other game" players are gracious—and tip well.

Without exception if you wish to be known as a lady or gentleman and a skilled "other game" player, you will exhibit courtesy, polite gracious behavior, and show your appreciation to those in service positions by thanking them personally without condescension, and tipping generously when they perform well.

There is no excuse, nor room in the "other game" for ungracious, unseemly, unbecoming or unkind behavior.

Principle #23

"Other game" players avoid giving golf lessons.

Finding that you are a more skillful golfer playing with others whose skills are of a lower level, avoid giving them any pointers or "golf course lessons." until the end of the round—if at all.

They usually don't work, and are better left to the practice tee.

In the event *you* are the experienced player, playing with a less-skilled or even a novice player who's an "other game" player, your mission requires being patient and allowing your novice partner to enjoy a pleasurable, well-paced day of golf. To this end, encourage their pace-of-play, and avoid correcting their sure-to-be-faulty techniques.

Principle #24
"Other game" players maintain 19th hole decorum.

Playing the 19th hole requires no clubs, golf shoes, balls, handicap, or caddie. Here, over a beverage, strokes evaporate and scores drop; memories grow fonder as successes loom larger. The swing is shortened—you need only one arm

And while the 19th hole is indoors, unlike the other 18, it's a place of opportunity for your informal business development to continue post-round, over a snack or a meal, and libation.

With any pressures of your game dismissed, and relationships cemented, this is where you plan your next get-together. Here, you or your playing partners may segue into the underlying purpose for this golf outing—business.

Avoid over-indulgence. Doing business sober is not only easier, but makes a far better impression. It also means a safe drive back to the office or home.

When things have gone well, whether you've discussed business formally or not, create the opportunity for a *social* commitment to get together at some future time.

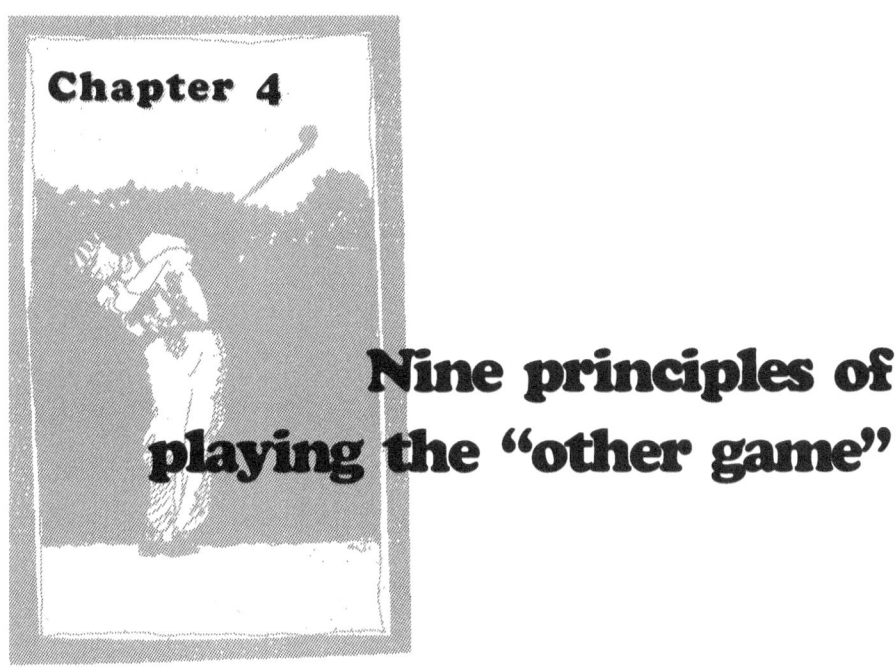

Chapter 4

Nine principles of playing the "other game"

Your objective is to fully experience the course, much in the manner of an artist, or writer, drawing on the course as an inspiration, as if it were a blank canvas or page.

This sounds esoteric, but bear with us because what we're describing is not a methodology, or a set of how-to instructions. It is far more subtle, and thus more difficult to articulate and grasp.

Imagine looking at a round in the same way an artist "sees" a picture before it is created. By orchestrating and blending the shapes and forms with color, a series of single brush-strokes is transformed into a painting.

"Other game" golfers see, or visualize the round before they play and then deftly step into it. They enter in a state of mental disengagement, or non-attachment that allows them to play even when a stroke is inept or imperfect.

Playing without attachment to success or failure, you simply remain in the picture you've created—the game. In this realm of the game you are unfazed by what others—if they have noticed at all—will soon forget. This leaves *you* open to anything that may come up for *them*. This is your form of *magic*.

We all acknowledge that golf can be a difficult, challenging game, where no hole is ever played the same way twice. But it is *because* of the elements of uncertainty—the variables including weather, equipment, personalities—that no game is ever the same. This unique set of circumstances belongs only to you and your golf companions at this time, on this course, under this sea of sky.

You are all here to play and enjoy the game, whatever the outcome. What can really be wrong? You're on a golf course on a beautiful day. You're not on a battlefield, in a hospital, a morgue, in court or a grim jail.

Be grateful.

Principle #25

"Other game" players enjoy walking the course.

When conversation lags due to mid-afternoon fatigue, take advantage of a wonderful, hoary old golf tradition. Climb out of the cart, take a few clubs, and walk.

Suggest your playing partners put a few clubs under their arms and walk the fairways with you.

Repeat this for a couple of holes. Trade off driving the cart. Notice how conversation starts picking up when your blood starts flowing. Golf, in its original and truest sense was meant to be walked and the ball to be played as it lies, "down."

At some point every golfer who wants to master the "other game" will do this.

Walk the course often, practice and play with the ball down; it's a discipline that will without question make you a better golfer.

Golf was made for walking, cart or no cart.

Principle #26

"Other game" players take advantage of cart time.

Players may spend several hours together in a cart while playing a round of golf.

The protocols start when you first climb into the cart.

Etiquette demands that the host usually drives. The host/driver's clubs belong on the left side. Same-side bagging can save a lot of time on the course, and keeps club exchanges smooth.

If the host has never played the course, the player most familiar with the golf course should drive.

Before you leave the first tee, familiarize yourself with the course driving rules. On public and private courses, course rangers can eject you from the course for failing to follow course rules.

Golf carts are not go-carts. Most have governors and can't be driven over a few miles an hour. Don't try power slides around downhill sloping turns over a wet cart path. Drive respectfully and sanely.

When a course has strict rules, respect them. Stay on cart paths whenever possible. Some courses, such as Pebble Beach, require that you stay on the cart path throughout your round.

Principle #27
"Other game" players regulate pace-of-play.

Golf is an enjoyable game; make sure you and your playing partners never feel rushed or hurried.

To orchestrate this, observe their various levels of skill, and regulate your pace-of-play accordingly—regardless of your playing ability.

Expedite by observing this important formerly unwritten rule: *never slow down your group*—under any circumstances.

When you slow down, you automatically slow any groups playing behind you. Potential clients, or executives you're courting, finding themselves forced to wait for you on the course may conclude that they could well be waiting for you in business.

Avoid this at all costs.

Principle #28

"Other game" players play promptly.

Play promptly without rushing your partners or the game.

This is accomplished by being mindful.

Be prepared, club in hand, and ready to hit your ball when it's your turn. Then, mark scores on the next tee.

To do this consistently, remain aware of where your ball is at all times and those of your playing partners as well, in the event that their attention has lapsed and they haven't followed their shot.

Initially, playing with this kind of pace may seem awkward. With practice, however, it will soon become rhythmic.

Should you make low score on a hole, be ready to tee off first on the next tee. If you are not a long hitter and you are playing with long hitters, go ahead and hit once the group ahead is out of your range, this will promote faster play.

Principle #29

"Other game" players avoid making others wait.

Prompt play relates to how much time it takes to play.

Prompt play is not associated with better players, nor is it related to the level of play or the number of shots.

Develop a mindful awareness of your role in the pace of play during your next round. Attempt to keep the flow of the game constant so that no one in your group or the group behind you is waiting for you.

Next, after a couple of rounds of this kind of awareness of keeping up the flow, notice how much easier it is to get around a course.

What's appropriate in pursuing prompt play always depends on the situation. One simple technique that will maintain the flow of the game is watching your ball.

Avoid becoming miffed when you hit a shot and forget to follow the ball. Should this occur, and should you not see the ball land, and it didn't appear to be heading towards a lateral hazard, hit another ball.

This will save you having to walk back to the where you hit the first shot to hit another.

Alternately, let your playing partners know, drop one and make up your own penalty with their acknowledgment. Circumstances are unimportant—when you're playing, play.

Save practicing for the range.

Principle #30

"Other game" players avoid holdups.

Avoid being the one who holds up or is holding up the foursome.

Requiring other golfers to wait is inexcusable.

Originally, golf was made to be played using an honor system: i.e., the one who is farthest from the hole hits first.

Always, without exception, be prepared to hit/play when it's your turn. This will assist the game-flow, and keep the pace-of-play up as well as everybody's spirits. Golfers find it very disruptive to the pace-of-play when the person farthest from the hole and designated to hit, passes up their turn.

Principle #31

"Other game" players avoid playing therapist.

Finding yourself with a playing partner who's showing signs of stress, anxiety or emotional turmoil—avoid playing psychotherapist.

We live in a time when business and stress are synonymous—so never underestimate anxiety. It will walk right out the office door, climb into your car, sit on the bench in the locker room as you change, and proceed to make itself a not-so-unseen companion on the round.

So again, resist any impulse to play psychotherapist.

What you can offer is *supportive* non-verbal communication—creating a spacious, relaxed silence. Eventually your partner will relax enough to begin conversation.

Remember: don't problem-solve. Just listen. Nod your head. Be supportive without offering solutions. And if you can learn to play this part of golf's "other game," regardless of your handicap, you will be a winner a thousand times over.

Principle #32

"Other game" players know bad games may have good results.

Even a disastrous game may be a successful business move and save countless hours and untold dollars.

After playing a round with a particularly bad-natured or boorish person whose course demeanor and lack of social skill portends a difficult business relationship, you may choose not to carry your business relationship beyond the course.

Think of the time and dollars you'll have saved—as well as having avoided making a business enemy.

Certainly playing a round of golf and discovering a potential client or boss's shortcomings is a far cheaper—and more pleasurable—method than having a contract sour or getting passed over, somewhere down the line.

Principle #33
"Other game" players avoid initiating business discussions.

As a practitioner of the "other game," your mission is not doing the talking but being an active listener.

Listening is one of the best ways to forward a conversation on and off the course.

As a listener, you'll have a much greater sense of when speaking is appropriate.

Should you want to talk about something business-related on the course, let the other person decide whether they want to talk about it or not. Some people never discuss business on a golf course. Others can't wait for the opportunity.

Remember, we're discussing principles—not technique. If there is a right way of bringing up business on a round when the subject hasn't come up before, we haven't discovered it.

What we've discovered is that you'll know when the time's right—when you listen.

Chapter 5

Seven principles of social strategy

Authenticity and mindfulness are primary keys to success.

The more authentic you are, the more you respect yourself and those around you. The more mindful you are, the more space there is for relationship and business opportunity—while not talking *about* business.

Suppose you are on the first tee with a potential client who is capable of generating considerable fees for you or your company. Would you even think of asking if they can use your services before you hit your tee shot?

Unlikely, and certainly inadvisable—let alone on the first hole. But since you both do business, it is more than likely that an opening will occur sometime during the round.

J. Paul Getty emphasized that one of the most important keys to being successful in business was to be relaxed.

Avoid trying too hard.

Principle #34

"Other game" players are social initiators.

Initiators make connections, and look for games.

Playing in tournaments, team play events, making a foursome, or putting on a tournament are all great ways to network.

Suppose your company doesn't have an annual tournament. Is there any reason you can't create one? It doesn't matter who does or doesn't play. Have it at a pitch-and-putt. The point is to get people together in an atmosphere of fun.

That's the way you begin to play the "other game" of golf.

Principle #35

"Other game" players are don't wanters.

"Other game" players understand that inviting people to play a round of golf with someone whom they'd like to do business, or conversely, being invited by someone they suspect may want their business, requires nothing more on their part than enjoying the round.

They have mastered the most subtle social skill of all—being a don't wanter.

A don't wanter requires nothing more from the game than knowing—if they are hosting—that their guests are enjoying themselves. A don't wanter's guests' most important obligations are letting their host know that they're enjoying the round and the company.

A don't wanter can simply relax and play the game. If business topics, or wagering come up, s/he can offer or respond with grateful interest, or decline with appreciation.

Wagering etiquette is simple: *Avoid initiating a bet. Wager only when asked.* "Other game" players never want to appear as if they're somehow trying to hustle a few exta dollars.

This don't-wanting attitude allows "other game" players a distinct psychological advantage. They can simultaneously be grateful without incurring obligation, and discriminating without being offensive.

Principle #36

"Other game" players love an enthusiastic player.

People enjoy playing golf with players who show their enthusiasm for the game—not because they hit the ball a certain way.

Skillful players of golf's "other game" create ways in which they can forward business relationships, professional or personal; not necessarily at that moment, but at some point in the future.

By being sincerely enthusiastic about your game—no matter your level of skill—you will encourage others to share their enthusiasm with you.

Principle #37
"Other game" players avoid becoming golf introverts.

Golf's "other game" as we mentioned in our introduction, requires developing an adroit synthesis of psychological, athletic, and business/networking skills. Fundamental to the "other game" is developing a habit of playing with other people.

Going to a driving range, hitting balls over in the corner of the range, isolating, and never playing or mingling with other people is not conducive to mastering the "other game."

If you have any intention of becoming an "other game" golfer, avoid becoming an introverted range player.

Principle #38

"Other game" players are alert for opportunity.

Your cubic centimeter of opportunity starts with your two-or-foursome's members.

On occasion fortune smiles. You've just been provided an opportunity to discover who the people you work for, or with, really are, their varied backgrounds, likes, dislikes, what and whom they deem important in their lives.

You now have four or five hours of their time, without haste or interruption, to create a series of opportunities for your fellow golfers to talk as much or as little about themselves as they like. Even a casual inquiry about wagering can tell a lot about a player's skill-level.

And this is the key. People, and successful people in particular, enjoy sharing their success.

Listen to, and learn from them. Create the space for them to enjoy their game. They'll appreciate how you've contributed to the round—regardless of your level of skill.

Principle #39
"Other game" players avoid defining wants as needs.

Avoid defining your golf objective or goal as a "want."

Defining what you *need* from business golf is of primary importance, once you've committed to the extent of taking lessons, buying clubs, and purchasing a golf wardrobe.

We don't always believe subconsciously that we *deserve* what we want. But we almost always know, and therefore get, what we *need*.

So, ask yourself, "What is it I *need* from my business game?"

Once you have defined your need, then you can structure your golf practice to meet that need.

And remember: *"Wants are wishes; needs are met."*

Principle #40

"Other game" players observe their partners' playing levels.

Learn how to recognize the three levels of business golf—casual players, active players, and committed enthusiasts.

A casual business golfer plays business golf from one to five times a year and rarely plays much beyond this level.

Casual players usually avoid such things as ongoing lessons and regular active practice, relying instead on an "I'll hit a bucket before the round," approach.

Casual players are usually quick to admit that their game is "not very good." And it's easy to see why they end up filling foursome gaps in scramble tournaments.

Active players play anywhere from six to 12 times a year, practice on occasion, perhaps play in a tournament, and play for enjoyment as well as business. This player was probably once more active, but is now playing less frequently due to family demands or time constraints. Actives are often rated as above average golfers, shooting with an under-20 handicap.

Committed enthusiasts, by contrast play two or more times a month, mixing both pleasure and business. Actives usually belong to a private or public club, and regularly use golf to entertain clients or contacts. Their scores will range from a scratch golfer (no handicap), to a 20-handicap, and they tend to play best at their home club.

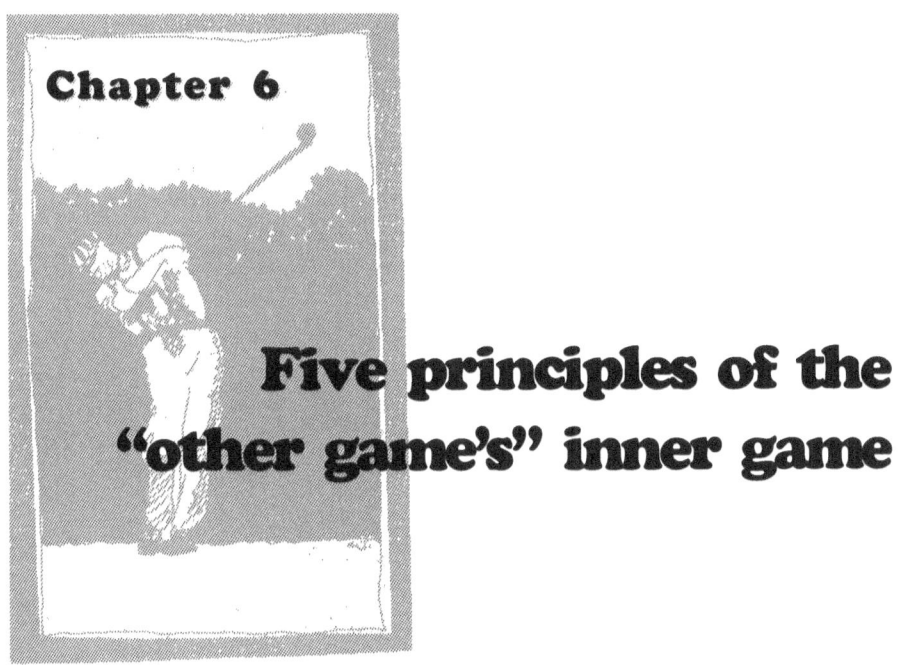

Chapter 6

Five principles of the "other game's" inner game

The **Other Game** *of Golf* is an inquiry into business golf designed to increase the level of enjoyment and interaction you—and those with whom you play—derive from the game.

Because this is an inquiry, our strong emphasis is not on technique. We're interested in perception and perceptual skills.

Golf, as a game for life, demands both time, and a certain level of dedicated effort to develop satisfactory playing proficiency.

Stop thinking about "getting" anywhere. You have already arrived. You have all the equipment—arms, hands, feet, eyes, central nervous system, and a brain that makes them all function together. What you need are a few provisions for the journey. You'll need *intent*, and *the ability to live in and enjoy the moment.*

This means using what skills you've acquired as best you can, relaxing, and having fun.

If there is any formula to preparation it's essentially this: prepare mentally, prepare physically. Maximize your time spent practicing and improving those areas of the game which will provide you with improved skills and scores—in the shortest amount of time.

If you deem your "other game" important, you will structure in lessons and practice, not on an *"Oh, God, gotta game coming up with an important client. Gotta look good. I'd better cram some lessons and practice in this week,"* basis, but important enough to structure your life so there is time for the activity, sans *urgency*, and the concomitant stress that invariably accompanies urgency.

Structured in this manner, no matter what your level of skill, seeing a golf teacher on a regular basis will be both beneficial and efficient.

Schedule lessons on a once-a-week, once-a-month, once-every-two-months basis. *When* is not important. What is important is that you plan on doing this on a regular basis, *creating* it—not as a rushed getaway from other activities or a crowded agenda, but a carefully and very consciously designed part of your own *life plan*.

The benefits will soon become apparent—not in terms of immediately realizable success in scoring, but in terms of your ability to make fewer mistakes.

Principle #41

"Other game" players define themselves as magicians.

Define your role, either as guest or host, as the "gracious magician" who makes the game flow, and strives to make it comfortable and pleasurable for everyone.

Create your magic through visualization.

Visualization is simply a mental rehearsal of all the situations surrounding the anticipated round. This simple psychological technique will allow you to truly play golf's "other game."

Visualize everything: the initial meeting; practice at the range and putting green; breakfast or lunch; all 18 holes of the round; even the 19th hole.

Any specific things you want to do or say over the course of the day can be visualized—to your benefit.

But be flexible. As a don't wanter remember not to be obsessive and attached to forcing something over the course of the round just because you thought it would be useful in the pre-game visualization.

Skillful "other game" players—since they are always interested in forging strong personal bonds—waste no time being concerned if their partner is unable or unwilling to discuss business.

Interesting subjects are never in short supply.

Principle #42

"Other game" players make arrangements in advance.

"Other game" golf always starts before the game, with the invitation, scheduling, and confirmation of a round.

This is less a matter of strategizing than of simply being aware that if the opportunity arises you have made your socially gracious magic, by doing some planning in advance.

Principle #43
"Other game" players call the pro beforehand.

As a host who has invited others to play an unfamiliar course or club, call ahead to get specific directions.

Contacting the pro or his assistants with a phone call or fax can open up your group to the possibility of a warmer reception when they arrive.

Are you a guest? Ask them to send you get a copy of the course layout beforehand. Fifteen to 20 minutes of study before of the round will unquestionably make you more competent and allow you to focus on creating a relationship with your host and the rest of the group.

When hosting at your own club, or favorite course, make sure your guests have good directions. Sending or faxing a map will put them at ease and reduce their anxiety over finding the golf course.

Principle #44

"Other game" players befriend starters and caddiemasters.

On occasion "other game" players may have plans disrupted by unanticipated emergencies.

Severe traffic, cancelled flights, or some other unexpected event are often less dramatic but equally discommoding contributors to this kind of inconvenience, leaving you minus one or more of your playing partners, perhaps even the guest you considered the most important.

At times like this, you may need help in improvising. Here starters and caddiemasters will often assist by suggesting substitutes, and adjusting tee times.

It's axiomatic that any leverage you have with a caddiemaster or starter is directly proportional to how well you are regarded on the course you are playing.

Principle #45

"Other game" players avoid economic surprises.

When you invite others to play, make their status as either your paid, or "Dutch" guests clear.

Most business golfers expect to pay their own way regardless of the type of course, nevertheless, you want to avoid a situation where someone is unclear about the arrangements.

Going Dutch—sharing the round's expenses—is acceptable under many conditions, but remember to make sure that you know the costs and disclose them well before the round.

If you plan on picking up the green fees, pick up the cart as well. The last thing you want to do is have your unsuspecting guest digging in his pockets for his share of the cart fees.

It's less-than-gracious, and bad form.

PART II

Putting Golf's "Other Game" Into Play

"Other game" principles in action

Chapter 7

"When the student is ready the teacher appears."

Playing the "other game" requires a realistic assessment of the level of playing skill you'll need to achieve.

Is shooting an 80 a realistic goal for you when you're only playing five to ten times a year? Remember, you—as an "other game" golfer—define *your* goal for *your* game.

Perhaps you are only able to play ten times a year at this stage in your business career. Is that a problem?

When defined as a negative—"How can I ever improve when I can only play once every six weeks?" it becomes a *limitation*.

Defined as a positive—"I plan to take at least six lessons this year, and to play once a month regardless of my schedule"—it then becomes a plan, a program, and a way to look forward to improving your skill-level with a conscious directive.

Lessons require a teacher, and while there are many good and even great teachers, finding one whom you can afford and from whom you can learn is the next step.

In seeking a teacher remember: *The best teachers teach us to teach ourselves.*

Presuming that you know little or nothing of the game, your first step may be to master a basic understanding of the rules and fundamentals of stance, grip, backswing and downswing.

So how often should you take lessons?

Since those of us in business put great value on time, ask yourself, "How important is improving?" Then discuss a schedule with your teacher.

And avoid limiting your play to driving ranges.

Chapter 8

Practice, practice, practice

Once you've learned the rudiments, nothing's more important for the beginner than just practicing swinging the club and hitting the ball.

Practicing on a driving range offers a low-cost venue, in contrast to a golf course. Hitting a bucket of balls is relatively inexpensive, depending on the range. Ranges vary from artificial turf mat, to live grass. But remember our earlier cautions that they are limiting.

During your early phases of learning, you'll find it easier to hit from a mat, due to the surface consistency. Grass driving ranges will provide a more realistic hitting surface, however, so be prepared to move up, and pay a few dollars more.

Most golf clubs have practice areas where you can pitch and putt, and these are good environments in which to practice, as well as study how other people present themselves, behave, and handle their equipment.

Since hitting the ball and keeping it in play define successful golf, your "other game's" physical skills will be adequate when you can advance the ball with reasonable consistency.

Chapter 9

Into the game—feet first

Beginning golfers need basic equipment for the game. This includes appropriate attire, golf clubs, balls, golf gloves, bag, and shoes.

"Other game" golfers tend to take notice of touches such as a nice pair of well-cared-for golf shoes.

Purchase good, name-brand shoes from manufacturers such as Foot-Joy, Etonic, or Nike. Make sure that they are *roomy*, *comfortable*, and *durable*.

Most golf shoe manufacturers offer golf shoes that have a treated leather upper and a rubber sole, ideal for damp early morning, or wet play. If you select the always popular saddle-shoe styles, select belts that match or compliment the saddle's color. And keep those saddles well-polished if they're smooth leather.

Women may need more than one pair of golf shoes to accommodate their golf wardrobes which tend to reflect seasonality more than men's typically basic wardrobes. Men's and women's golf shoes vary considerably in price.

In the past we've preferred shoes with screw-in spikes, finding them more desirable, however, sole technology improves constantly, and today many courses will require that you wear spikeless shoes.

Be prepared to adjust accordingly.

Chapter 10

Provisions for the journey

To start your journey into the realm of the "other game" you'll need basic golf woods including a matching driver or 1-wood, and a 3-wood.

Your first clubs need not be top-of-the-line. It's also possible—with careful shopping—to buy acceptable used woods at considerable savings.

For new clubs, expect to spend much more. However, keep your initial club purchase minimal and simple. A 5-wood, for instance, is a useful tool, but not necessary for the beginner.

Shop for basic irons, 2-through-9, and a pitching wedge. New top-of-the-line Callaway's or Ping's, are very expensive, however, so be aware that as a beginner you can purchase a less-expensive and perfectly serviceable new set that will suffice for the first few years.

Discuss your purchase of clubs with your teaching pro, or an experienced golfer you trust—before you buy any clubs. They may be able to offer useful insights.

Used Clubs

For a beginner working with a limited budget, used clubs can save substantial dollars, however it is important to know what you are looking for. New, or good used clubs can be found at a reasonable cost. Most name-brand clubs are safe, as long as they are steel shafted. Graphite shafts must be inspected carefully, as they can deteriorate with hard use and improper care, and a beginner tends to be rougher on clubs than an experienced player

While high-end clubs can cost thousands of dollars it rarely benefits the beginning business golfer to spend the maximum for clubs. Experienced players become suspicious when they see an obvious beginner hacking away with custom-fitted top-of-the-line Callaway woods and irons. The message they receive is that this player is pretending to be better than s/he actually is.

When purchasing used clubs, *caveat emptor.* Make sure that the clubs are a known brand, of recent design, and in good shape.

When considering used clubs, examine the grips and the shafts. Avoid purchasing worn or bent clubs. Also, avoid exotic or unusual designs unless you know enough to know that they'll they work well for your game. We suggest graphite shafts and metal heads for woods.

When you start looking you'll quickly discover that clubs come in two varieties: name-brands vs. imitations—knock-offs. Today, every name-brand club like Taylor Made, Callaway, Cobra, or Ping has been imitated. Since most clubs are cast from a mold, it is easy and inexpensive for a company to manufacture clubs that are almost identical in design to those of major manufacturers. Component materials in the club heads are equal or similar; most differences, however, will be found in the shafts, and the workmanship with which the clubs are assembled.

There is an observable level of craftsmanship involved in making high quality brand-name clubs that separate them from the lesser brands and knock-offs.

If you are serious about the game, spending several hundred dollars more for a set of clubs over a three-year period is a justifiable expenditure.

Putters

Putters come in all shapes and sizes. Don't obsess about exotic equipment. To get started, find a relatively conventional putter and learn proper putting technique. After this, test a few at your local golf shop before choosing.

Putters vary in price, but the most important factor is selecting a putter with which you feel comfortable. Evaluate several. If you find one that allows you to sink more putts—this is the one worth spending more dollars on.

Selecting a putter is far more subjective than selecting woods or irons. Due to the delicacy of the putting stroke, your putter has to be your friend—or your ability to make decent putts will be limited.

If you are consistently playing on public courses which tend to have slower greens, we suggest using a somewhat longer, heavier putter. This will allow you to get the ball to the hole on slower greens.

For faster greens select a lighter, shorter putter. A lighter putter gives more feel and sensitivity.

Let common sense be the arbiter. Use what works. Remember that most great putters can see a line—an imaginary path from the putter and the ball—to the hole.

This should be something that you can make sure you do before you decide to buy a new putter to replace the old. Once you have a putter and it doesn't seem to be working, don't look for a new one until you have looked in the mirror for a while to determine what needs changing.

Balls

Golf balls, like rabbits, seem to mature rapidly and multiply.

Remember, the ball is your *scoring* implement. Always show up with at least one new sleeve of golf balls, preferably with a known brand.

Avoid using X-outs, or old bag-balls if you can help it.

Beginners should select a more durable covered ball, and advance to a higher-control ball like a *balata* as their game progresses. Surlyn® balls are substantially more durable and will travel farther than a balata. We suggest using a Surlyn for handicaps of 10 or more. If you are a 10 or less, we suggest using a balata but not necessarily sticking to one.

If you are a low-handicapper and still fail to hit the ball very far, it may benefit you to compare the two kinds of balls to see which works best.

Surlyn goes farther, supporting a short-hitter's game. A long-hitter profits by the balata's touch.

Bags

Even though most golf is played with a golf cart, select a bag that is lightweight with an adequate neck for the clubs to slip in. Make sure you have at least one large pocket, necessary for carrying a sweater, shoes, umbrella and various necessary items.

Should you occasionally plan to walk the course, consider purchasing a lightweight carry-bag. Lightweights are less bulky to transport.

If you do a little smart shopping and keep an eye for pro-shop sales, you may be able to pick up two bags for the price of one.

Chapter 11

Correct attire for the "other game"

For men in business, dark suits, laundered shirts, and silk ties have been the standard, traditional, metropolitan uniform. In recent years, however, the casual business-look has crept into mainstream business, especially on Fridays.

Golf attire has evolved from neck-tie formal in the early years of the 20th century, to shirt-sleeves-and-necktie, with tweed or flannel slacks and a tweed golf cap during the 1920s and 30s, to a more casual look in the post-war 1940s that has become today's standard.

Contemporary golf has retained and fostered this traditional-yet-casual look, with the exception of an odd fling influenced by the disco-era-polyester 1970s.

In golf, classic tends to remain classic. Knee-length Plus-fours worn with long Argyle stockings were first introduced and became fashionable in the late 19th century.

Today, Plus-fours are decades out-of-fashion, but still in style, worn by the English and Scottish gentry on courses in England and Scotland and occasionally in the US on exclusive private courses and by certain professionals. When correctly tailored and worn—often by distinguished-looking mature players such as the Prince of Wales—they appear elegant, and stylishly classic. Here is a perfect example of the difference between style and fashion.

Broad or narrow contrasting horizontal or vertical stripes or patterns, for instance, may be in fashion one year and out the next. Basic solid colors, including navy blue, white, Hunter green, olive, or gray, may not be "in fashion" but never go out of style.

Unwritten requirements of the "other game"

Golf is a tradition-directed game, and as a savvy business golfer, no matter what your level of skill, you'll want to cultivate a high level of sensitivity to the "other game's" unwritten requirements.

Basic golf course apparel for men currently consists of golf slacks or clean, pressed khakis and a comfortable, appropriate, short banded-sleeve polo-style, or plain-sleeve golf shirt, with a collar. With variations this will probably continue well into the next century.

While polo shirts, golf slacks and khakis have become casual golf-wear standards these items can vary in price and quality. Slacks are a good example. They can range from under fifty dollars to over three hundred.

Gloves and Belts—men

Pick gloves and belts to compliment shoes. Tan leather or combination leather and fabric gloves will match brown or tan bucks or saddle shoes. Select belts in the same range of colors.

Gray flannel or worsted golf slacks and a well-made expensive polo shirt matched with white/black saddle shoes and a dark belt and dark windbreaker make a more formal combination.

Caps and Visors

Match your golf cap or visor to your shirt. When in doubt, always pick solid, conservative colors.

Dress Codes

Certain private courses have stringent dress codes, including requiring collars on shirts, no shorts for men, and recommended short lengths for women players. A quick call to the club's pro-shop will provide you with the dress code. Don't forget to make it.

Avoid Levi's

Avoid Levi's, denim jeans, or jean-cut trousers.

Avoid novelty items, including funny hats.

Avoid t-shirts with large logos or designs on the front or back.

Avoid outrageous plaids or loud clashing colors.

Well-schooled gentlemen "other game" players tend to avoid any jewelry with the exception of class or wedding rings, and wristwatches.

Avoided by astute "other game" male aficionados are visible gold neck chains.

Avoid visible religious medals or symbols. The exception would be a golf-playing member of the clergy.

Women, however, may use tasteful jewelry accents.

Appear unencumbered. Avoid fanny-paks, pouches or gadgets that attach to your belt.

Keep simplicity in mind.

Cooler Days

For cooler days, ladies and gentlemen should layer with a lambswool, cashmere, or one of the synthetic fleece pullover sweaters or a vest, and a roomy windbreaker or windshirt. Keep a lightweight nylon rain-parka folded up in your bag, and a golfer's umbrella, or at the least a collapsible traveler's umbrella.

Chapter 12

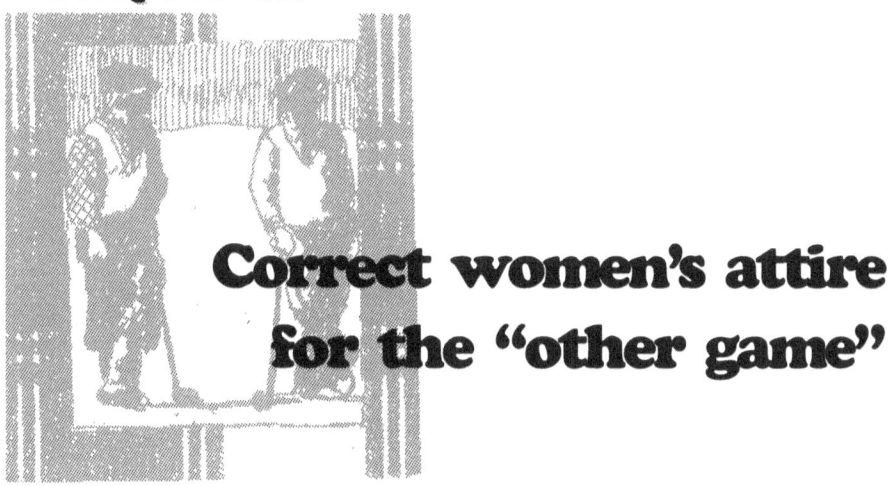

Correct women's attire for the "other game"

Women, as reflected in your business attire, enjoy a much greater latitude in their golf activewear. Most women have a far better-developed color-sense than men, and are more sophisticated and adept at picking and including varied fabric and color combinations.

There is only one significant rule: avoid unusual, or bold attire.

You are allowed knee-length shorts on all courses, as well as tailored golf skirts, or slacks.

For summer play, pick collared golf shirts that will give you adequate skin protection on hot, sunny days, and allow good air circulation.

As with men, have a warm sweater, vest or cardigan for cooler days, a light jacket, windshirt or a rain-parka with hood or some sort of suitable cover. This will serve to protect your hair in the event the weather turns inclement, and can be stored in your golf bag.

Avoid shirts without collars, tank, halter or tube tops, short skirts, aerobic outfits, and Lycra tights or tops. Remember the "other game" requires a more conservative outlook.

Add a low-key sweater for cool rounds, and comfortable golf shorts for hot days.

Chapter 13

Words of wardrobe wisdom

Since golf is not a casual sport, it has never shed its special feel or appeal.

Reflective of this is the fact that at this writing, golf professionals are wearing better-designed, more conservatively styled clothing for the game. Whether this is a trend remains to be seen. Fashion designers, and sportswear manufacturers with a need to create sales and turnover in their various garments lines, can be counted on periodically to parade and promote unbelievably tasteless wares.

Fashion is commodity, and commodities are marketed to sell. The serious student of "other game" golf understands this, and resists spurious fashion.

Appropriate Attire

Attire—and the impressions your golf attire create—is very important. The PGA, for instance, puts so much emphasis on appropriate attire that it requires professionals wear long pants, not only at their home course, but even while visiting, practicing, or playing on another course.

Golfers playing the "other game" know that they have just one opportunity to make a good first impression. From a business perspective, it is important to be appropriate in selecting and wearing appropriate golf attire.

Create a versatile golf wardrobe that works for a variety of climate and weather conditions. Since weather can change dramatically over the course of a day, be prepared for hot, cool, and potentially rainy days.

When you start to play frequently, buy and keep an extra of pair of shoes available. Should one pair get wet, you'll have a back-up. And, of course, keep them clean and well-shined.

Comfort

We recommend dressing as comfortably as you can in loose clothing that will not inhibit your swing, while still retaining a well-coordinated sense of style.

Select good natural-fiber slacks such wool gabardine or tropical worsted. They are always appropriate. Light tan, cream, or light gray are basic, and will mix with any other combination of shirt colors. White is less desirable, and black is not recommended.

Khakis, made of 100% cotton drill or twill are almost always appropriate and can be dressed up or down as the occasion requires. Lightweight cords will also fit the "other game's" requirements.

Shorts

Shorts are acceptable on most courses today, and if you play with partners who themselves are wearing shorts, and you look well wearing them, don't hesitate—with one exception for some men of Caucasian extraction. If it is early in the season, wear slacks until you have gradually—with sunscreen—tanned some color in your legs.

For men, well-cut khaki twill or drill shorts are always acceptable. Beyond this, little can be said. Other colors and materials come and go and are transitionally acceptable.

Again, remember the distinction between the "other game" and pure social golf.

Golf Shirts

Three-button traditional polo-style shirts are always acceptable.

Short-sleeved 100% cotton button-down collar, button-front sport shirts in solid pastels, Tattersol, or Madras plaids are acceptable. These are comfortable to wear, especially during the hot summer months.

Newer fabrics, which are blended and woven to provide greater air flow, are becoming increasingly available. Always remember to buy shirts of a generous, relaxed fit that won't magnify sweat stains.

Sweaters

For cooler mornings, fall days, and late afternoon games long-sleeved sweaters serve well without inhibiting your playing form. Knitted wool vests are also comfortable on days when the temperature drops just below short-sleeve comfort.

Men should remember to match their sweaters with their shirts and slacks.

Windshirts

Windshirts, or light hooded parkas, serve both to insulate from a whipping wind as well as protect from light rain. They offer resistance to the elements without heavy layers to affect your swing. Stylish, they can be an added element to your golfing ensemble. If there is some question about weather over the course of a round, a windshirt can be a welcome addition to your bag.

Some players find hoods impossible to play in. A light, foldable brimmed rain hat is a welcome addition.

Rainsuits

Rainsuits are light and waterproof. Golfers who actually have one tend to play a lot, and are unfazed by inclement conditions. A rainsuit's advantage comes when the sky opens up; you'll be able to continue your round without returning to the club to scrounge up foul-weather gear, or sit out the storm.

Hats and Caps

Hats provide protection from the sun, and insulate the head on colder days. Baseball caps, visors, and wide-brim floppy hats are typical. Logos from golf manufacturers, or clubs, and tournaments are popular and acceptable.

Well-schooled "other game" players always wear a clean hat during business golf. Just because it's lucky doesn't mean it can't be clean.

Real luck can't wash off.

Chapter 14

Zen and the art of "other game" maintenance

Applying Zen to golf's "other game" is straightforward:

> *Playing golf well requires consummate awareness.*
> *Appreciate the opportunity to play.*
> *Treat the course well.*
> *Care for your equipment and wardrobe .*
> *No exceptions.*

People who care about their lives and take their sports seriously, care well for their equipment.

When your grips become hard, wash them thoroughly. If your grips are rubber or a synthetic composite, soak them in hot, soapy water and take a fine wire brush and lightly scrub all the surface areas of the grip. Then take a towel and squeeze and twist them dry. They will feel as good as new, if not better. Follow this routine every third round when you are playing consistently.

Wipe down shafts with a good silicone-impregnated fishing-reel cloth. Wipe grass and mud stains off your bag.

Treat leather grips or the leather parts of bags and gloves with saddlesoap, Lexal® or another good brand of leather preservative.

Chapter 15

Keeping "other game" behavior on course

How should you act on the golf course?

Quietly, respectfully and calmly.

Everyone knows the Golden Rule; we've coined the Greens Rule: *Do unto others on a golf course as you would want others to do with, or for you.*

Following this simple dictum will make for a better game—with or without playing partners.

Skillful "other game" golfers know that the way people behave on a golf course may be an indicator of the way they behave in life, and business.

Being ready to hit when it's your turn, raking the bunkers and replacing the divots are simple, considerate activities that show respect for the game, and for the course.

And when players follow these rules, act with respect towards the course and the game, we have a good indicator of how they will behave in other areas of life.

We all learn as children that behavior affects the perceptions of others toward us. On the course it may dramatically affect your future business relationships.

Suppose you set up a golf game with a potential client and before the round you establish a bet for the day. On the 18th green you are one-up, and your companion has a 4-foot putt to win the hole and tie the match. The putt swings wild. The potential client starts whining and pleading with you that the putt was so short that it was good.

Would you feel comfortable doing business with his person if s/he is doing this over a golf bet? How are they going to be in business, and can you afford to find out?

Opportunity's Cubic Centimeter of Chance

Perhaps by luck—as the firm's most junior member, or the division's newest addition, or as an entrepreneur of accumen and business skill—you are asked by the higher-ups to join them for a round, or at a company-sponsored charity tournament.

Appropriate opening topics include simple questions about gear—shoes, clubs, and bags. If you're a beginning golfer, or have never played this course—you're in a wonderful position to request tips and inside information on the challenges this particular course presents.

In the event you have invited your companions, and you are familiar with the course, the reverse holds true. You can become their guide.

Your fellow player's answers will often relate experiences on their favorite courses, and aspects of their backgrounds as golfers that are keys to their personalities.

Waiting, perhaps while the foursome ahead plays through, gives you a chance to ask more questions. Are your companions from out-of-town-or-state, what colleges did they attended, and of course, how long they've been playing golf?

Older players may have had some interesting military service, or taken recent trips abroad.

Beyond this you can discuss the world at large, *with the standard social exceptions of partisan politics or religion,* unless you find that you all share the same political or religious views. Not that political or religious issues must be avoided *per se,* if they come up, but listen carefully, and keep in mind that your mission isn't an ideological or religious conversion, but developing a business relationship.

Chapter 16

Game combinations, clubs and courses

Golf's "other game" identifies three basic game-combinations or situations, including the twosome, foursome, and tournament play.

Twosomes are very informal; typically this is one of the better opportunities to discuss business, due to the setting.

Foursomes, depending on if you are playing with familiar or new companions are somewhat more formal, and represent a less-opportune time to discuss business.

Tournaments are the most formal, depending on the type of event. Discussing business may prove more difficult.

Here you may need to shine as a competitor, a worthy opponent and a team member. Focus on making the best shots for your team.

Playing Public Courses

If you are just starting out and don't belong to a private club your option is to begin your "other game" career by playing on public courses. Public courses are acceptable—but remember to secure a *convenient* starting time prior to making your invitation. Then contact your targeted players:

"Hi, John. This is Brian. I'm getting a foursome together for the fifteenth at Convoluted Knolls. Starting time's eight-thirty. Right, it's a Wednesday. The weather? Been terrific and we'll probably have the course to ourselves seeing as it's St. Nobody's Day and there's a parade downtown. Remember my mentioning Bob Brown from Computeq? Right, he's joining us, and I'm looking forward to having you meet him."

Chapter 17

Join a club

Your objective in playing golf's "other game," is to develop relationships with certain business people. Depending on your profession or line of work, golf and country clubs are a great foundation for networking. Whether a doctor, or lawyer, accountant, sales, or a small business owner, the information and services available to a club member can prove invaluable.

Needless to say, country club memberships don't come cheaply. Your ability to join a club will be in direct proportion to your income, and the amount you deem important enough to spend or set aside to join a club.

Fortunately there are some very good and affordable alternatives.

Public Course Clubs

Many public golf courses offer a men's/women's club memberships. After paying a standard nominal fee for establishing a club membership, the new member is then rated and distinguished as a handicap golfer, becoming part of a loose organization around the club. Reasonable monthly fees allow you a limited number of guests and access to tournaments.

You'll benefit from a public golf course club membership by preferential time access, and lowered round fees, benefits which border on the country club membership.

Country Clubs

Joining a country club is both more costly, and difficult.

Joining a country club also means being *invited* to join, which can take time. Joining requires cultivating members, being sponsored, and going through the nomination process before finally joining.

Vetting, or being selected for an equity-membership, may depend on a variety of factors including length of the list of applicants, your sponsor's clout with the board of directors and selection committee, and other never-admitted-to factors including race, ethnicity, and social position.

During periods when memberships have dropped off applicants may be vetted in quickly—at substantial savings over those times when membership lists are crowded and potential members are willing to pay premium prices.

The immediate benefits of country club membership include exclusivity, accessibility, and reciprocity. The subtle benefits include a substantive status boost among your peers who play golf, but don't belong to a country club.

Since country clubs typically have limited memberships, you'll enjoy significant perks, including more flexible tee times, and the aforementioned reciprocity agreements with other clubs. Club pros also have tacit reciprocity agreements among each other, and this means you have access to an even larger golf-intelligence network.

Types of Memberships

Memberships vary, but are usually of the equity or non-equity type. Typical of prestigious clubs, equity memberships signify an equity position in the club, and generally cost more.

Junior memberships are offered at many clubs for players between 25 and 35 years of age. The cost differential can be considerable, deferring up to 75% of the total membership fees. At a club where a membership costs $100,000, but only $20,000 for a junior membership, $80,000 is deferred until the junior member either joins and pays the balance as a full-fledged member at a certain age, or pays incremental fees over a period of time until membership is sustained.

Expect to pay monthly fees and dues, and to be assessed for a variety of club-related improvements over the life of a given membership.

And never, never, never, fail to pay your dues on time.

Word gets around.

Chapter 18

Prestigious Golf Clubs Observe Formal Rules

In most cases, prestigious golf and country clubs observe more formal rules of behavior.

One of the more commonly observed formalities is the avoidance of using cash—except for tipping. Tips, however, are frequent and generous.

When you've been invited to a club like Augusta, or Bel Air for a specified tee time, arrive at least one hour early.

Exclusive clubs have a bag drop area where players leave their clubs. Inquire at the gate, and then drop your clubs, with the attendant. Park, and request directions to the gentlemen's or ladies locker rooms.

Take your tote-bag with your golf clothes and shoes, and request a locker from the locker room attendant.

In the event guest lockers are unavailable, either check your business attire with the attendant, or leave them neatly under the bench in your tote-bag.

Most clubs have restrictions regarding the wearing of golf shoes in specified areas. Before leaving the locker area, inquire about club rules.

And always remember to tip—generously.

Chapter 19

Prestigious Golf and Country Clubs' 19th Holes

As we've previously observed, prestigious golf and country clubs observe more formal rules of behavior.

As a novice golfer who is a guest at such a club, you should be aware of the protocols. After the round, for instance, etiquette demands that the club member offer the guests an option to shower. Should they decline, players may simply have a drink and some food, socialize, or finalize business discussions, then shower before leaving. However, if the day has been hot and the players would be more comfortable in dry clothing, a shower may make the 19th hole more enjoyable.

Never attempt to pay for drinks or meals at a private club. Not only is it impossible to pay with cash or credit card, it's inappropriate—you're the guest. Save your treat for your turn as host.

Avoid bringing any business materials with you to the table. Many clubs frown upon or prohibit any formal business discussions. Should you need to note important information, discreetly note it on the back of a business-card or a napkin.

Don't be surprised when you see notable business people or celebrities socializing at the club's 19th hole.

Should you recognize someone you know, take a moment to acknowledge them, with a nod, smile or wave—but don't over-do it. It reflects poorly on your social skills, and reduces the importance of your host. Table-hopping is not only unprofessional, it shows a profound lack of courtesy.

Be gracious and inquire if your host knows your acquaintance who may be a member or a guest. Generate an easy introduction.

Perhaps you notice a business acquaintance sitting with friends, playing cards. First, inquire if your host knows your friend. If the host says "yes," you have the option of making an introduction or simply acknowledging your acquaintance with a nod, wink, wave, or gesture.

If your host doesn't know the other person, wait until an appropriate time, and make a friendly introduction. Avoid overdoing it with other familiar club members. It reduces the intimacy of your special outing. However, letting your host know that other club members are friends or acquaintances may be an advantageous move.

This rule also applies for hosts. Perhaps your guest has never been in a club like this before, and might be feeling somewhat uncomfortable.

Avoid spending an inordinate amount of time socializing with other club members while your guest sits idly by. Introduce your guest first, and make your guest feel important instead of uncomfortable.

Chapter 20

Wagering

Some of us, due to our upbringings, or specific religious or moral beliefs find ourselves, as beginners learning to play the "other game" of golf, confronted on the course for the very first time, with the confusing dilemma posed by wagering.

Or, perhaps we have simply never gambled, or even played card games, and our unfamiliarity with the process of betting makes us feel uncomfortable. Take heart.

What we quickly discover is that betting changes the round. Betting golfers tend to be *very* competitive.

Betting is an acquired taste. It can also be confusing. Certain bets require complex calculations. For beginners it's perfectly acceptable to politely decline, or ask for an explanation of how the bet works. *"Thanks for the offer. I'm just learning. How does this bet work?"*

If you are a beginner be prepared to lose $5 or $10, and enjoy it. Here are three simple guidelines:

Be aware that betting increases the pressure of competition with your fellow players.

When you accept a bet, determine how much you can afford to lose—and make sure you can cover it.

Retain sufficient dollars—for food and drinks.

Remember golf is a game dictated by social decorum—jungle or no jungle out there.

In the metaphorical jungle of the genteel, rules and decorum are observed with consummate grace as the metaphorical carcass is torn to pieces.

Types of wagers

Nassau is a *match play* wager that is divided into three bets, one for the back nine, one for the front, and one for the total 18.

When you hear: *"I'll play you five dollars three ways."* This is a Nassau bet: $5 for the front side, $5 for the back side, $5 for the total.

If someone asks you to play $5 four ways that means that the 18th hole bet is double, or worth $10.

Often players will want to play this bet with "2-down automatics," meaning that anytime a player gets 2-down, a new bet starts. *Watch out, this is where it can get expensive.*

Rabbits are bets that are broken down for every six holes. A player wins the "rabbit" by having the most legs at the end of the six-hole stretch.

A rabbit is scored by beating the other players on a hole—this gives you a leg. Win three legs, and you automatically win the rabbit.

To hold onto your legs you must, at the very least, tie the other players on the following holes.

Skins consists of each player shooting for low score on each hole. Lowest score on a given hole wins and gets a "skin." Skins are worth from $0.25 to $50.00.

At the end of the round the players add up their total number of skins, and each pays-out accordingly. This is a classic wager because no matter how badly you are hitting, you'll always have a chance to win on the next hole.

When you decide to wager, make sure you understand the bet. Never, under any circumstances, rely upon your opponent to figure it out for you as it makes you appear incompetent.

For the More Experienced

"Other game" golfers, depending on their level of skill, may find they enjoy having a little juice added to the game. But be aware that what is appropriate for some business rounds, may be inappropriate for others. Etiquette is simple, remember Principle #35: *Avoid initiating a bet. Wager only when asked.*

As a rule of thumb, when hosting less-experienced players make wagering friendly, and explain how the bet works.

Initially it's better to suggest a low dollar wager. Don't overwhelm your partner with complexity. A $2 Nassau can provide just enough to make it fun—as opposed to painful.

Chapter 21

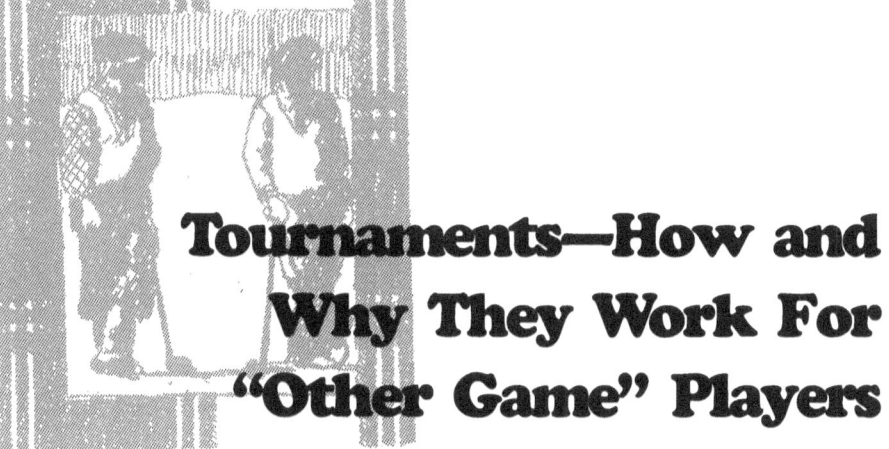

Tournaments—How and Why They Work For "Other Game" Players

Novice golfers can and should begin playing in tournaments, especially industry "best-ball scrambles."

In a four man best-ball scramble, a foursome hits their shots and moves forward to the "best shot" of the group, while scoring only the group's best shots. These tournaments are great, both for novice and experienced golfers, because the format encourages team effort and quick play.

Summer vs. Winter Rules

Tournaments generally dictate playing by either *summer rules*—you play the ball where it lies—or *winter rules*—you may move the ball, no nearer the hole, but within six inches of where it was.

Summer rules are tougher. Off of the green, you may not touch the ball.

When you play in an association, club, city, state, or national event, you will probably play summer rules. During events sponsored by corporations, charity events, small events, or company retreats expect to play winter rules.

Playing in groups you will likely agree before the round under which rules you will play. Higher handicappers often favor winter rules, while lower handicappers tend to prefer summer rules.

Of course, if the course gets too wet even the best players will move the ball.

Tournaments Offer Opportunities

Tournaments offer the "other game" golfer a setting conducive to enhancing relationships and establishing new contacts. Understanding the nature of the various tournament formations will allow you to direct your energies accordingly.

Tournaments include Pro/Am, (professional/amateur) charity, industry, and club events. Formats vary from gross or net formats, to best-ball, scramble, and "one club" events.

Pro/Am Tournaments

Pro/Am events usually precede a professional event like the Los Angeles Open. There are differing systems of play, but usually the tournament is a one-day format, with individual scoring used to determine winners. Amateurs are paired with pros over the course of a round of golf.

Pro/Am tournaments are usually very costly, but they may also provide a major opportunity for business development

Here, the "other game" golfer must have no more than a 15 handicap—and shoot accurately under pressure because of crowds on the course observing the participants. Every shot off the fairway becomes an opportunity to hurt someone.

Pro/Am tournaments like the Bob Hope allow celebrity amateurs and corporate golfers of Fortune 500 companies to play for multiple rounds over the course of the event.

Charity Tournaments

Charity tournaments are designed to raise money for a specific charity, and provide general access to new contacts. Usually these are some type of best-ball format, where all who play participate equally. Charity events provide an excellent opportunity to make points with a prospective client with an invitation to be your guest for the day. The costs might be rather high, but you can be assured that your guest will perceive this to be a prestigious invitation.

Ancillary benefits include meeting other high-level members of the business community before and after the tournament.

Industry Events

Industry events afford the best access to others with common business interests. These tournaments are organized as leisurely days dedicated to enjoying the golf course, and interacting with others. Be prepared. Ask others to set up a foursome, or invite other players to join your group.

Volunteering as a tournament chairman allows you contact with industry leaders over an extended period. This takes a substantial time commitment, however, and the success of the tournament rests on your shoulders.

If the tournament is going to be a large production featuring 25 or more players, select a good committee to assist in developing the tournament. This will save headaches and time as the tournament nears. Also, find someone you are cultivating to assist—and avoid burdening your secretary—unless she wants to enter.

Tournament Formats

Your tournament format will be determined by the anticipated number of entrants. Smaller tournaments of less than 100 players tend to run sequential tee-off times. This means that groups will be playing over a longer period during the day, making it more difficult to have meaningful interaction before or after the tournament. Groups will be spread over a three- to four-hour period for tee times in this manner.

Shotgun tournaments are preferable as an industry format because they allow a large number of golfers on the course at the same time. Players start simultaneously on different holes on the course, and some tournaments are even held on two sister-courses located at the same facility.

Important things to consider for the tournament format are how many good golfers—those of less than 10 handicap—are in your industry group. Good golfers tend to enjoy playing best-ball events over scramble events because they resemble a true round of golf.

The most popular formats are gross and net divisions:
1) 2-man best ball
2) 4-man best ball
3) 4-man scramble

Costs for a tournament game vary according to a variety of factors. The inclusion of breakfast or dinner, or both, is not only a good idea, but a smart one. In the event the meal is served in a nearby hotel, or at the club, you've just created another opportunity to enjoy new company, and learn about them. Events which include meals are usually appreciated because they generate cohesion, fill hungry stomachs, allowing any necessary announcements to be made to the assembled group under sit-down conditions.

Alcoholic beverages should be a discretionary item for tournament golfers. A drunken golfer makes a lasting unprofessional impression. Save the drinks for the 19th hole.

Door prizes are important especially for those golfers who love accumulating things at tournament. Depending on the type of event you hold, prizes may be solicited and donated by people on your committee.

In the event you have an advertising agency as a participant, ask them to donate the logo-workup, an attractive graphics package, and all the artwork to create embroidered caps, visors, and golf shirts.

Picking a charity is a wonderful idea to help promote your tournament. This lets everyone feel good. Some very large tournaments have grown from modest beginnings to large events due to well-established women's charitable organizations affiliating with the event. Often celebrities will support charitable causes in the name of golf. These people are not difficult to enlist if you are helping a high profile charity.

As we've noted, club tournaments can be helpful in developing potential business contacts, but this environment must be viewed as a long-term method. Few club players will feel comfortable discussing business with you during these events unless you are an insider. Remain low-key during club events and concentrate on building relationships and good will.

Corporate business development is also possible for sponsors of major PGA tour events, and large corporations have been using this technique for years

These sponsorships can be as simple as daily tournament passes and hospitality tables within a tournament—at thousands of dollars per day—to specially designed entertainment chalets for up to 100 guests and 18th green sky-box access, costing hundreds of thousands of dollars.

Under these impressive conditions, guests can enjoy a day at a very prestigious tournament, and business development may become an all-day affair.

While very expensive, the impression on the guests will be remembered and appreciated.

Chapter 22

Tipping Caddies

Tipping, in any situation, is regulated by the amount of appreciation the recipient of a service shows for the level of service another has performed.

There is really no set dollar amount that applies to all situations in golf. Savvy "other game" golfers finding themselves at a club where they've never played before will usually inquire about the standard tipping rate from the pro, or a member.

Don't be embarrassed or reluctant because you're a newcomer; simply state the facts.

"I've never played here before, and I'd like to know the going tip rate for your caddies."

They'll tell you, and you can incrementally adjust that dollar figure up or down according to the caddie's performance.

Always tip caddies according to their performance.

Chapter 23

Pace-of-play and Other Important Factors

Pace-of-play is always important, cart or no cart. Of course the *tempo* of the round will depend on whether you are walking or riding. Little nuances that speed-up play include using the "Three Club Rule."

Remain aware of your part in the tempo of a golf round; it will create a subtle impression on your business companions.

Always leave the cart with two or three clubs in hand.

This allows you to avoid going back and forth from the cart to your ball.

When in doubt as to your ball's location, hit a second ball.

Always keep an extra ball in your pocket, so that you are not trekking back and forth to the cart or having to ask your playing partners.

If your playing partner is about to hit, and your ball is +/- 40 yards away, go to your ball before he hits his shot and be ready to hit.

This saves tremendous time and gives you both an opportunity to talk after the shots.

Unless you are betting, and you've taken eight swipes at the ball and its still not in the hole, pick it up and cuddle with it until the next tee.

Your playing partners will thank you for it.

Should you notice another player in your group doing this, perhaps you could suggest, with enormous diplomacy and tact, the above-mentioned action to avoid emotional displays and club-throwing.

Public Courses Are Slower Than Private Courses

Public courses tend to play more slowly than private courses due to the greater number of players.

This volume simply slows the overall round down. In this case, the length of time it takes you to play a round of golf is out of your hands, and the only thing you can control is the time spent during a hole—by eliminating others waiting on you.

Slow public course rounds are those with tee-off times between 9:00 A.M. and 1:00 P.M. Playing an early morning 6:00 A.M. round where your group is one of the first-off for the day, you may find yourselves playing at a three-and-a-half hour pace.

Under these circumstances you are going to want to keep their pace, not yours.

Watch Where You Stand

Avoid stepping in other people's lines of sight.

Never stand directly on the other side of the hole from where someone is putting. Watch your shadow. Avoid allowing yourself or your shadow to be seen—even out of the corner of their eye.

Wrapping Up

Changing focus from on-course discussions of pin placement to private placement will seem much easier, because you and your companion have just conquered, or been conquered by the course.

Over a cool drink or warm meal you can sense how your relationship has progressed. It's a simple matter to change focus from the game to the relationship.

Chapter 24

Establishing Your Handicap

Golf, alone among games, developed an equalizer to allow golfers of varying skill levels to play together and challenge each other. The system is called the *handicap* or *index*. Handicaps function as a recognized, legitimate measurement of a golfer's current skill-level.

Golf courses are one of the few places on earth where a handicap is not a negative, but an equalizer, leveling the playing field. With a handicap, a game of golf is mutually available to an enthusiastic 12-year old or a top touring professional. The handicap allows them to actually play together—competing from their own levels of skill against the difficulty of the course.

Every state in the country has a golf association where players can establish handicaps. Currently, the newest handicapping system, *slope rating* is established by calculation. Once established, your handicap will vary according to the course you play.

If you putt and hit reasonably well when not under pressure, but tend to fold when stakes are added—such as betting, or playing in a tournament—your handicap will probably not serve you as well at those who consistently perform well under pressure.

111

How Handicapping Is Abused

"Sandbagging" is the not-so-polite term used to describe a player who establishes a higher handicap that misrepresents his ability in order to play with an unfair advantage in tournaments.

Tournament officials—wise to the trick—are now using players' tournament scores to establish handicaps.

Chapter 25

Putting Promotes Points

Your ability to score favorably in the "other game," is achieved by mastering score-lowering tactics.

As a novice, practicing putting will improve your game more than any other activity. While less physical and exciting than wood or iron shots, putting accounts for one-half of all scoring. This makes putting easily the most valuable element of the game.

Being able to two-putt consistently is the fastest way to break the "100" scoring barrier, and thus feel comfortable playing golf's "other game."

Warming Up

Putting is the most important warm-up you can have before a round. It's easy to forget that putting is half the game, and taking 10 minutes to warm up is extremely useful to making the most of your round. Practice five or more long putts of 30 feet and finish with a half-dozen 6-foot putts. By starting with the long putts the 6-foot putts will feel very easy and establish a relaxed rhythm.

Chapter 26

Why Golf Was Made For Walking

Remember Principle #25: *"'Other game' players enjoy walking the course."*

Don't deny yourself the opportunity, to spend time walking the course—regardless. More than one "other game" golfer has told us that simply taking the time to walk the course had the salutary effect of a spiritual experience.

A CEO of an electronics firm recounted his experience while walking the Los Angeles Country Club's North Course.

"I've done my share of time in church, but never have I felt so close to God as I did that afternoon. I couldn't tell you just what came over me. I have no words in my vocabulary to express the peace and beauty that I felt—except to say that it was truly spiritual. Spiritual."

At this point our CEO lifted his eyes in what could only be described as a reverential gesture. "It wasn't something that I'd prayed for, or even anticipated. It was just a wholesome, complete, positively charged period of time that was—well, like a communion."

To him, at this time, neither score nor other players mattered. He was transformed from a man with huge cares, responsibilities and worries to being a mindful, aware individual. He had found a temporary respite, peace in a place that evoked his response—his communion.

Chapter 27

Ensuring Prompt Play

Playing golf's "other game," means it isn't important if you are a 2-handicapper, or you can hit a ball 300 yards; what's important is that you keep up the pace or flow of the game.

Suppose you're playing with a potential client, an important supplier whom you are attempting to attract to your packaging business.

You simply don't want that prospect having to wait for you throughout the round. His or her impression of your pace-of-play may be the impression that goes back to the board of directors.

Here is one way to insure this doesn't happen. We call it the *ball-in-your-pocket dictum*.

Train yourself to carry an extra ball in your pocket and, as we've previously recommended, carry two or three clubs when leaving the golf cart so that you won't find yourself returning to the cart to get an extra ball or to change clubs.

Many public courses are cart-path only, requiring golfers to walk some distance to the ball from the cart at the side of the fairway.

When in doubt as to locating your ball—hit a provisional ball instead of disappearing into the rough.

Now, when you carry that extra ball in your pocket, you've just eliminated trekking back to the cart to get another.

Remember what we advised before: *when your playing partner is about to hit his fairway shot and your ball is +/- 40 yards away, go to your ball before he hits his shot, and be ready to hit, saving time and giving you both an opportunity to talk after shooting.* No doubt your partner will be more than happy to describe the "great shot" over and over again.

Chapter 28

Drinking, Smoking, and Eating on the Course

When drinking, smoking, or eating, behave appropriately and respect your playing partners whatever forms their indulgences may take.

You will experience times, especially during tournaments, when a good deal of alcohol may be consumed during the course of play and after. Here it is best to carefully pace your intake. As we've stated elsewhere, golf's "other game" requires keeping your wits about you. You're not here to unwind, but to have fun while establishing and fostering stronger personal relationships.

Smoking

Smoking has become a sensitive issue, on or off the course.

Smoking is a psychologically and culturally complex behavior, and one that deserves some attention for the "other game" golfer.

In the United States today, smokers find themselves increasingly curtailed and the freedom of an expansive golf course may offer them tacit permission to relax and indulge in their habit.

Since most Europeans, Middle-easterners, and Asians smoke, as visitors they may react with perplexity when encountering that self-righteous breed of American—the self-appointed Tobacco Police.

Conversely, you may be a non-smoker who finds smoking offensive so be aware, *if your partners are smokers, that it is in your best interest to let them enjoy their cigarettes or cigars, regardless of your own attitudes toward smoking.*

Should your partner relish a fine cigar, consider purchasing a premium cigar to offer after a few holes as a gesture of camaraderie. Cigar aficionados will recall the gesture with pleasure.

If you have any doubts about the appropriate brand, check with a local cigar shop prior to the game, and purchase a selection. Spending a few extra dollars for premium cigars will be well-appreciated. People remember simple acts like this; they are seen as clues to the "other game" golfer's character.

With respect to extinguishing your smoking materials, be careful. Never throw a lighted cigar or cigarette out of your cart. Use the ashtray—just as you would indoors.

In the cart or on the green, take care and extinguish it and either field-strip your cigarette or cigar butt, or put the extinguished butt into a trash receptacle. Burning down the 5th hole won't further your reputation in the business world.

Etiquette for snacking is simple—*bring enough of anything you wish to consume, and offer to share. And never, never, never litter.* Not the smallest of wrappers, or the tiniest piece of trash. Pack out what you pack in.

During the course of the day, you may have the opportunity to enjoy a variety of items, soft drinks, chips, candy bars, sandwiches. Appoint yourself the cart caddie, and prevent things from flying out and littering the course.

Again, little embarrassments are best avoided.

Chapter 29

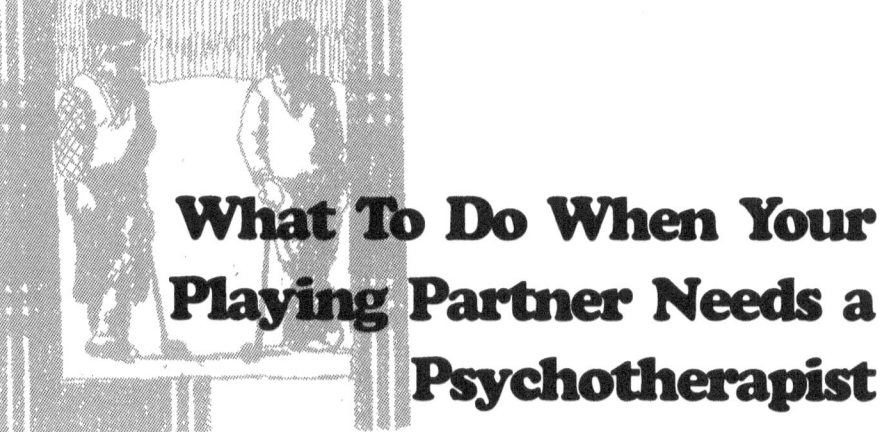

What To Do When Your Playing Partner Needs a Psychotherapist

Perhaps as you tee off you notice that your partner is intently focused on his game, and while perhaps not lock-jawed silent, s/he is far from loquacious. There may be any number of personal or business-related stresses occurring in his life.

Men, in life and business, often deal with their problems by distancing themselves from the source of anxiety.

Most of us, men and women, think we disguise anxiety and stress better than we actually do. Just because you've reserved a tee time, arranged for a great foursome, done your pregame visualization, and practically have the deal put together in your head—don't think that will relieve stress—yours or theirs—automatically. It may take some skillful means to create that particular kind of relaxed harmony that makes for a great round of golf.

Here, most women enjoy an enormous advantage. They are generally more emotionally sensitive and empathetic than men. When they encounter a male playing partner who's facial expression resembles a razor clam at low tide, most women will read the signs faster than men.

Remember, girls grow up watching their fathers and brothers. They learn from an early age to match their responses to tense or depressive male behavior, diffuse the male's anxiety and make normal conversation the next step.

This technique is especially good for men who find themselves playing with a woman partner who's under stress unrelated to the game.

Offer solutions only to men. Women don't want solutions—they prefer empathy.

Conversely, while most men don't mind if their female playing partner notices or even remarks that they have something on their minds other than their game—the last thing in the world men want is their *male* playing partners noticing that they're experiencing any stress or emotional discomfort. Males tend to consider this sort of behavior as a sign of weakness.

For men encountering this, your most appropriate response is to relax, directing your interest toward your own game, and offering a nod or smile when your partner's game is going well.

Chapter 30

Invitation and Reciprocation

Opportunities abound in any round of golf. Some, however, offer a greater range of possibility than others—especially when you receive an invitation to play at a prestigious club. Regardless of the situation, a little preparation will pay off handsomely here.

Invitations to certain places and events entail observing rules of protocol, etiquette, and behavior. These rules apply to both host and guest, and you should be aware that they exist.

Perhaps it's your first opportunity to meet with a potential prospect in his or her environment, or play a charity tournament with business leaders, or join a regular outing with business associates who play at your host's club.

Your ability to be seen as an appropriate guest is a measure of how well you have mastered golf's "other game."

Savvy "other game" golfers know that being a host and asking others out to play on their club's course puts them in a favorable position. Hosts, and hostesses as well, while appearing gracious and accommodating, enjoy both a feeling of pride, and the significant advantage of an effortless game on their home turf. Here, they are seen as insiders, who know and are known by everyone from the doorman to the starter.

Extending an invitation allows the host the distinct advantage and satisfaction of being the person in command of the round. The host is the guide who knows the course, and is privy to its anticipated surprises.

Perhaps you're from out of town. A considerate host will inquire if you have wardrobe, equipment, or need shoes. He will probably direct you to the club pro who will assist in compiling the necessary items.

Imposing Courses

In the event you are invited to a grand or imposing club such as Augusta, or the Congressional, it is acceptable as well as genuine to be impressed and delighted, especially if you have never been there before. Clubs such as these were designed to be impressive. Savor the experience, and your host will savor your response.

What is unacceptable, and unpardonable is to pretend, or act blasé. Such behavior is transparent and shows a distinct lack of sophistication.

How a Good Host Hosts

If your host or hostess is a well-schooled "other game" player they can be counted on to make sure you are provided with adequate directions to the course, the meeting area, and key persons who will direct you. Since you as a first-time guest arriving from out-of-town and unsure of directions may be anxious, the host's job is to turn that anxiety into a comfortable form of excitement and anticipation.

Experienced "other game" hosts will often send instructions with a map mailed or faxed a few days prior to the scheduled game. These may be as simple as a handwritten note or as sophisticated as a monogrammed invitation card replete with map, and directions to their club.

Upon arrival, a gracious hostess or host will inquire if you or the other guests have eaten, or would care for a refreshment prior to the round. If you need anything from the pro shop a gracious host will make sure the item is secured, and offer you the option of warming up on the driving range.

Experienced hosts are gracious, quick to put their guests at ease as they introduce them to other club members, staff, and the club's physical accommodations and traditions.

Experienced guests are charmed, delighted, careful to remember names and show appreciation without being obsequious.

With the game completed, "other game" guests show appreciation by a handwritten note, thanking the host for a great afternoon.

Thank You Notes Count

Understanding the rules of reciprocation constitutes an important if little-noted element of successful "other game" golf. While a truly gracious host or hostess would never count or keep a "thank you" score, considerate and thoughtful gestures of appreciation are rarely forgotten.

For business relationships to build, appropriate appreciation is critical. Short thank-you notes, letters, and cards are the basic elements you'll want to share. Timely response is usually within a week of the game. Most business people are impressed when response, even if brief, is immediate. If you discussed specific business possibilities, a professional letter on company letterhead should follow within a few days.

Epilogue

"*Manners*," Mrs. Lockwood, reminded us on more than one occasion, "*are not like a coat you can put on and take off.*"

Nor are these principles and suggestions for playing golf's "other game" themselves, like a coat. Rather, consider them as important structural components, a foundation for your successful journey into the adult realm of the "other game."

Once you have acquired them you'll wear them—forever. That's why we referred to mastering the principles as a *practice*, and this book as a *companion*.

A word to the wise, however; please don't expect to master complex social skills in one reading. Applying the principles will take considerable practice and mindfulness. There are, after all, 45 of them. So please avoid self-recrimination when the inevitable occurs, and you forget something. Excuse yourself, and move on.

Let the experience be a *reminder*, just as a badly judged shot can remind you to remind yourself to avoid making that same mistake again.

Simply make consulting your companion a practice.

About the Authors

J. Brian Amster has been an investment banker for 12 years, completing over 60 deals raising over $200 million for middle-market companies. He began playing golf 7 years ago after his colleagues invited him to play in an industry tournament. He searched for a book on the subject, and unable to find one, began developing the basis for The ***Other Game*** of *Golf*: Practical Principles & Strategies for Business on the Course. He now plays in 6–8 tournaments a year and regularly plays with professionals in the L.A. area.

Larry Salk owns and operates Ventana Systems, a distributor of electronic components, specializing in excess, obsolete and end-of-life material. He has been playing golf for over 26 years, and has been competing for 20 years playing in tournaments that include The Trans-Miss and California State Amateurs, and has tied for the course record-63 at The Chardonnay Golf Club in Napa, CA.

Craig Lockwood is an award-winning author and journalist based in Laguna Beach, California. His books, articles, photographs, and short fiction have appeared in magazines, and newspapers here and abroad. He has written for the stage and TV. Mr. Lockwood's upbringing stressed gracious good manners—on and off the course—as a foundation for success in life and business.

www.ingramcontent.com/pod-product-compliance
Lightning Source LLC
Chambersburg PA
CBHW030757180526
45163CB00003B/1057